Layers of Learning
Year Four • Unit Three

Industrial Revolution
U.S. Landscapes
Energy
Romantic Art I

Published by HooDoo Publishing
United States of America
© 2016 Layers of Learning
ISBN 978-1534970434

Units at a Glance: Topics For All Four Years of the Layers of Learning Program

1	History	Geography	Science	The Arts
1	Mesopotamia	Maps & Globes	Planets	Cave Paintings
2	Egypt	Map Keys	Stars	Egyptian Art
3	Europe	Global Grids	Earth & Moon	Crafts
4	Ancient Greece	Wonders	Satellites	Greek Art
5	Babylon	Mapping People	Humans in Space	Poetry
6	The Levant	Physical Earth	Laws of Motion	List Poems
7	Phoenicians	Oceans	Motion	Moral Stories
8	Assyrians	Deserts	Fluids	Rhythm
9	Persians	Arctic	Waves	Melody
10	Ancient China	Forests	Machines	Chinese Art
11	Early Japan	Mountains	States of Matter	Line & Shape
12	Arabia	Rivers & Lakes	Atoms	Color & Value
13	Ancient India	Grasslands	Elements	Texture & Form
14	Ancient Africa	Africa	Bonding	African Tales
15	First North Americans	North America	Salts	Creative Kids
16	Ancient South America	South America	Plants	South American Art
17	Celts	Europe	Flowering Plants	Jewelry
18	Roman Republic	Asia	Trees	Roman Art
19	Christianity	Australia & Oceania	Simple Plants	Instruments
20	Roman Empire	You Explore	Fungi	Composing Music

2	History	Geography	Science	The Arts
1	Byzantines	Turkey	Climate & Seasons	Byzantine Art
2	Barbarians	Ireland	Forecasting	Illumination
3	Islam	Arabian Peninsula	Clouds & Precipitation	Creative Kids
4	Vikings	Norway	Special Effects	Viking Art
5	Anglo Saxons	Britain	Wild Weather	King Arthur Tales
6	Charlemagne	France	Cells & DNA	Carolingian Art
7	Normans	Nigeria	Skeletons	Canterbury Tales
8	Feudal System	Germany	Muscles, Skin, Cardio	Gothic Art
9	Crusades	Balkans	Digestive & Senses	Religious Art
10	Burgundy, Venice, Spain	Switzerland	Nerves	Oil Paints
11	Wars of the Roses	Russia	Health	Minstrels & Plays
12	Eastern Europe	Hungary	Metals	Printmaking
13	African Kingdoms	Mali	Carbon Chemistry	Textiles
14	Asian Kingdoms	Southeast Asia	Non-metals	Vivid Language
15	Mongols	Caucasus	Gases	Fun With Poetry
16	Medieval China & Japan	China	Electricity	Asian Arts
17	Pacific Peoples	Micronesia	Circuits	Arts of the Islands
18	American Peoples	Canada	Technology	Indian Legends
19	The Renaissance	Italy	Magnetism	Renaissance Art I
20	Explorers	Caribbean Sea	Motors	Renaissance Art II

3	History	Geography	Science	The Arts
1	Age of Exploration	Argentina & Chile	Classification & Insects	Fairy Tales
2	The Ottoman Empire	Egypt & Libya	Reptiles & Amphibians	Poetry
3	Mogul Empire	Pakistan & Afghanistan	Fish	Mogul Arts
4	Reformation	Angola & Zambia	Birds	Reformation Art
5	Renaissance England	Tanzania & Kenya	Mammals & Primates	Shakespeare
6	Thirty Years' War	Spain	Sound	Baroque Music
7	The Dutch	Netherlands	Light & Optics	Baroque Art I
8	France	Indonesia	Bending Light	Baroque Art II
9	The Enlightenment	Korean Peninsula	Color	Art Journaling
10	Russia & Prussia	Central Asia	History of Science	Watercolors
11	Conquistadors	Baltic States	Igneous Rocks	Creative Kids
12	Settlers	Peru & Bolivia	Sedimentary Rocks	Native American Art
13	13 Colonies	Central America	Metamorphic Rocks	Settler Sayings
14	Slave Trade	Brazil	Gems & Minerals	Colonial Art
15	The South Pacific	Australasia	Fossils	Principles of Art
16	The British in India	India	Chemical Reactions	Classical Music
17	The Boston Tea Party	Japan	Reversible Reactions	Folk Music
18	Founding Fathers	Iran	Compounds & Solutions	Rococo
19	Declaring Independence	Samoa & Tonga	Oxidation & Reduction	Creative Crafts I
20	The American Revolution	South Africa	Acids & Bases	Creative Crafts II

4	History	Geography	Science	The Arts
1	American Government	USA	Heat & Temperature	Patriotic Music
2	Expanding Nation	Pacific States	Motors & Engines	Tall Tales
3	Industrial Revolution	U.S. Landscapes	Energy	Romantic Art I
4	Revolutions	Mountain West States	Energy Sources	Romantic Art II
5	Africa	U.S. Political Maps	Energy Conversion	Impressionism I
6	The West	Southwest States	Earth Structure	Impressionism II
7	Civil War	National Parks	Plate Tectonics	Post Impressionism
8	World War I	Plains States	Earthquakes	Expressionism
9	Totalitarianism	U.S. Economics	Volcanoes	Abstract Art
10	Great Depression	Heartland States	Mountain Building	Kinds of Art
11	World War II	Symbols & Landmarks	Chemistry of Air & Water	War Art
12	Modern East Asia	The South	Food Chemistry	Modern Art
13	India's Independence	People of America	Industry	Pop Art
14	Israel	Appalachian States	Chemistry of Farming	Modern Music
15	Cold War	U.S. Territories	Chemistry of Medicine	Free Verse
16	Vietnam War	Atlantic States	Food Chains	Photography
17	Latin America	New England States	Animal Groups	Latin American Art
18	Civil Rights	Home State Study I	Instincts	Theater & Film
19	Technology	Home State Study II	Habitats	Architecture
20	Terrorism	America in Review	Conservation	Creative Kids

Unit 4-3

Printable Pack

This unit includes printables at the end. To make life easier for you we also created digital printable packs for each unit. To retrieve your printable pack for Unit 4-3, please visit

www.layers-of-learning.com/digital-printable-packs/

Put the printable pack in your shopping cart and use this coupon code:

627UNIT4-3

Your printable pack will be free.

Layers of Learning Introduction

This is part of a series of units in the Layers of Learning homeschool curriculum, including the subjects of history, geography, science, and the arts. Children from 1st through 12th can participate in the same curriculum at the same time - family school style.

The units are intended to be used in order as the basis of a complete curriculum (once you add in a systematic math, reading, and writing program). You begin with Year 1 Unit 1 no matter what ages your children are. Spend about 2 weeks on each unit. You pick and choose the activities within the unit that appeal to you and read the books from the book list that are available to you or find others on the same topic from your library. We highly recommend that you use the timeline in every history section as the backbone. Then flesh out your learning with reading and activities that highlight the topics you think are the most important.

Alternatively, you can use the units as activity ideas to supplement another curriculum in any order you wish. You can still use them with all ages of children at the same time.

When you've finished with Year One, move on to Year Two, Year Three, and Year Four. Then begin again with Year One and work your way through the years again. Now your children will be older, reading more involved books, and writing more in depth. When you have completed the sequence for the second time, you start again on it for the third and final time. If your student began with Layers of Learning in 1st grade and stayed with it all the way through she would go through the four year rotation three times, firmly cementing the information in her mind in ever increasing depth. At each level you should expect increasing amounts of outside reading and writing. High schoolers in particular should be reading extensively, and if possible, participating in discussion groups.

These icons will guide you in spotting activities and books that are appropriate for the age of child you are working with. But if you think an activity is too juvenile or too difficult for your kids, adjust accordingly. The icons are not there as rules, just guides.

☺ 1st-4th
☻ 5th-8th
☻ 9th-12th

Within each unit we share:

EXPLORATIONS, activities relating to the topic;
EXPERIMENTS, usually associated with science topics;
EXPEDITIONS, field trips;
EXPLANATIONS, teacher helps or educational philosophies.

In the sidebars we also include Additional Layers, Famous Folks, Fabulous Facts, On the Web, and other extra related topics that can take you off on tangents, exploring the world and your interests with a bit more freedom. The curriculum will always be there to pull you back on track when you're ready.

www.layers-of-learning.com/layers-of-learning-program

UNIT THREE

INDUSTRIAL REVOLUTION - U.S. LANDSCAPES - ENERGY - ROMANTIC ART I

Waste no more time arguing about what a good man should be. Be one.
–Marcus Aurelius, Roman Emperor

LIBRARY LIST

HISTORY

Search for: Industrial Revolution, capitalism, labor strikes, Andrew Carnegie, James Watt, inventions

☺ ☺ ☻ Industrial Revolution for Kids by Cheryl Mullenbach. Includes comprehensive text and images as well as hands-on projects. Focused on the United States.

☺ ☺ ☻ Mill by David Macaulay. Intricate pen and ink drawings of a fictional mill in the United States at the beginning of the Industrial Revolution.

☺ ☻ The Bobbin Girl by Emily Arnold McCully. Fictional account of a young girl working in a factory. Will she join the union protest and risk losing her job?

☻ Henry Ford: Young Man With Ideas by Hazel B. Aird. Part of the excellent Childhood of Famous Americans series. Also look for John Deere, Booker T. Washington, Eli Whitney, and Orville and Wilbur Wright from this series.

☻ Lyddie by Katherine Patterson. Historical novel about a young farm girl who goes to the city to get a job in a factory to help her family.

☻ Invention by Lionel Bender. A DK Eyewitness book.

☻ Money by Joe Cribb. A DK Eyewitness book.

☻ The Industrial Revolution by Melissa McDaniel.

☻ Kids At Work: Lewis Hine and the Crusade Against Child Labor by Russell Freedman. Uses the photos of Lewis Hine to tell the story of child labor and the movement against it in the United States.

☻ ☻ Whatever Happened to Penny Candy? by Richard J. Maybury. Explains economic theories and money.

☻ Economics: A Free Market Reader by Jane A. Williams, editor, and Kathryn Daniels, editor. Essays by various economists about free markets. Easy to understand.

☻ The Autobiography of Andrew Carnegie.

☻ The Gospel of Wealth by Andrew Carnegie. This is sometimes included in his autobiography.

☻ I, Pencil by Leonard E. Read. An essay that explains how the many components of a pencil come together, involving diverse places of the globe and millions of people, all without any centralized creator. Explains the "invisible hand" concept of capitalism.

☻ North and South by Elizabeth Gaskell. Novel about class conflict, mill workers in northern England, and finding true love.

☻ The Most Powerful Idea in the World: A Story of Steam, Industry, and Invention by William Rosen. A history of the Industrial Revolution and why it started in Britain.

☻ Watt's Perfect Engine: Steam and the Age of Invention by Ben Marsden.

GEOGRAPHY	Search for: United States landscapes ☺ ☺ ☺ <u>Our Fifty States</u> by Stephen F. Cunha. From National Geographic, great photos, maps, and information for all ages. If you want to buy one book on all fifty states, this is it. ☺ ☺ ☺ <u>National Geographic Atlas For Young Explorers</u>. Worth buying. ☺ ☺ <u>A Walk in the Prairie</u> by Rebecca L. Johnson. See others in the "Biomes of North America" series by this author. ☺ ☺ <u>50 States: A State by State Tour of the U.S.A.</u> by Erin McHugh and Albert Schrier. This highlights a bit about each state and also includes a jigsaw puzzle of the states. ☺ <u>Across This Land: A Regional Geography of the United States and Canada</u> by John C. Hudson. A bit dense, but fascinating for the good reader. Explains how the physical geography of North America has affected its political and economic history.
SCIENCE	Search for: energy, potential energy, kinetic energy, chemical energy, pendulum ☺ <u>Energy Makes Things Happen</u> by Kimberly Brubaker Bradley. Part of the excellent "Let's Read and Find Out" series. ☺ ☺ <u>Energy: Its Forms, Changes, & Functions</u> by Tom DeRosa and Carolyn Reeves. Includes 20 hands-on projects that require some materials from a science supplier to complete. ☺ <u>Basic Physics: A Self Teaching Guide</u> by Karl F. Khun. Read chapter 3.
THE ARTS	Search for: Romantic Art period, 19th century art, William Blake, John Constable, J.M.W. Turner, Theodore Gericault, Eugene Delacroix, Francisco Goya, Hudson River School, Thomas Cole, Albert Bierstadt, George Stubbs, Thomas Lawrence, Caspar David Friedrich. You can pick up almost any art anthology and it will include a section on Romantic painting. ☺ ☺ ☺ <u>The Hudson River School: The Landscape Art of Bierstadt, Cole, Church, Durand, Heade, and Twenty Other Artists</u> by Louise Minks. This is a beautiful book that will help you love the first real art movement in America. ☺ ☺ ☺ <u>How To Paint Like Turner</u> by Nicola Moorby, editor, Ian Warrell, editor, Mike Chaplin, contributor, Tony Smibert, contributor, and Joyce H Townsend, contributor. This is an instructional book for anyone who wants to work on watercolor painting techniques. It is broken down into sections and gives guidance on a variety of techniques that beginners or advanced painters could learn from. ☺ ☺ ☺ <u>Turner: His Life and Works in 500 Images</u> by Michael Robinson. Images for all ages, text for high school and up. ☺ ☺ <u>The French Romantics: Literature and the Visual Arts</u> by David Wakefield. More advanced, but includes lots of pictures of the art from this period in France. ☺ ☺ <u>John Constable: The Making of A Master</u> by Mark Evans. This book accompanied a Constable exhibit, but you can enjoy the book on its own too.

HISTORY: INDUSTRIAL REVOLUTION

Teaching Tip

Timelines are especially essential during the modern period we're studying this year because so many of the units will cover the same time frame but focus on different events or different parts of the world. For example, during the Industrial Revolution we also have the Napoleonic Wars, revolutions around the world, the American Civil War, the rise of communism, the wild west, the land grabbing in Africa and more.

On the Web

This is an hour long video from the BBC about the Industrial Revolution: https://www.youtube.com/watch?v=CNOxCh-o7hWw.

Additional Layer

The Agricultural Revolution happened just before the Industrial one.

Learn more about this time and how it led to the Industrial Revolution.

The Industrial Revolution was the two hundred year period from approximately 1710 to 1910 when technologies were developed that changed society from an agrarian subsistence economy to a manufacturing urban wealth producing one. Many machines and technological inventions were produced like the cotton gin, steam engines, methods for extracting and refining ore, and internal combustion engines. The Industrial Revolution occurred in the Netherlands and in Germany, but most of it happened in Great Britain and in America. Capitalism and its attendant freedom, protection of property, and lack of government regulation provided the atmosphere where people could invent and be sure they would receive the fruits of their labor. It was a time that created a middle class, families who had more wealth and more luxuries than their ancestors had ever dreamed of.

This is the interior of Marshall's Flax Mill in Leeds, England. In a flax mill, fibers were spun into yarn for the textile industry. Leeds was a major manufacturing center during the Industrial Revolution. Notice that most of the workers were women. The picture was first published in 1843. Public domain

There were still problems though, including appalling working conditions in some factories and a shift from artisan labor to semi-skilled factory labor which left many without employment. A breakdown of the governmental role of protecting the life and health of people, especially children, meant that there were violent riots, protests, and massive political movements which reacted to capitalism with whole new philosophies. The labor unions and communism were both ushered in as responses to abuses.

In spite of the working conditions, people still poured into the cities looking for work. Immigrants from less free and more backward places poured into Britain and America looking for better lives. Most of them achieved it, if not for themselves then for their children.

☺ ☺ ☺ EXPLORATION: Timeline

Place these dates on your timeline. Printable timeline squares can be found at the end of this unit. We could have added many, many more dates, feel free to add more as you read.

- 1712 Thomas Newcomen builds first commercially successful steam engine which is used to keep mines clear of water.
- 1758 Threshing machine invented
- 1765 Thomas Hargreaves invents the spinning jenny for cloth weaving
- 1775 Watts builds a much improved steam engine
- 1779 The steam engine is married with the spinning jenny, creating the first industrial mills
- 1793 Eli Whitney invents the cotton gin
- 1801 Robert Trevithick builds the first steam locomotive
- 1811-15 Luddite riots destroy property and life in Britain
- 1821 Micheal Faraday discovers electromagnetic rotation, which leads to both electricity production and motors
- 1834 Charles Babbage invents the forerunner of the modern computer
- 1837 Samuel Morse invents Morse code and the telegraph
- 1838-39 Photographic paper invented by Daguerre and Talbot
- 1846 First pneumatic tire patented
- 1846 Transatlantic cable laid
- 1850 Process for refining petroleum first invented
- 1851 Singer invents his sewing machine
- 1859 Oil is first struck in Pennsylvania
- 1867 Alfred Nobel develops dynamite
- 1879 Edison invents the light bulb
- 1883 The first skyscraper is built in Chicago
- 1883 The Brooklyn Bridge is the largest suspension bridge ever built
- 1885 Benz invents the internal combustion engine
- 1901 Marconi first transmits wirelessly
- 1903 Wright brothers take first powered flight
- 1908 Henry Ford mass produces the automobile

Famous Folks

Charles Babbage invented a programmable computing machine, the forerunner of the modern computer, in 1834.

Additional Layer

Victorian London has a reputation for brutality on one hand and a hypocritical morality and refinement on the other. But how bad was it really? Look up stats on murder rates, poverty levels, education, charitable giving, and crime in general for 1890 and for today to compare.

On the Web

This 16 minute video explains the beginnings of the Industrial Revolution: how engines and the division of labor changed production and wealth:

https://www.youtube.com/watch?v=ntCVm-HENyOA.

Famous Folks

Look up these people and see what they invented.

James Hargreaves

Samuel Morse

Alexander Graham Bell

Thomas Edison

Nicolas Appert

James Watt

Louis Daguerre

Horace Wells

Charles Goodyear

John Dunlop

Thomas Newcomen

Isaac Singer

Cyrus McCormick

George Eastman

Nikola Tesla

George Westinghouse

Dr. Richard Gatling

Alessandro Volta

Writer's Workshop

Pretend you are a Luddite who is concerned with textile factories and other industries and inventions. What new things anger you the most? Write a letter to a friend telling your opinions and outlining a plan of what you will do about it.

On the Web

Video about Luddites:
https://www.youtube.com/watch?v=CNOxCho7hWw

EXPLORATION: Invention

This period was a time when invention upon invention was being added to the toolkit of mankind. Some of the most important include the steam engine, vulcanization process for rubber and thus pneumatic tires, anesthesia, refrigeration, photographic paper, telegraph, phonograph, light bulb, heat canning process for food, aluminum ore extraction, mass producing assembly line, spinning jenny for textile production, and iron smelting and steel production.

Choose one invention from this list or another that you know about and make a timeline of its invention, stretching back to the previous inventions that made it possible and to the future applications of the invention. Around the timeline write all the products you can come up with that use this technology or invention in daily life today. Add a caption box that tells the story of the inventor and his invention.

EXPLORATION: Inventor Biography

Select one of the inventors of the Industrial Revolution and research his life. Look at the sidebar to the right for ideas.

Write a biography or create a powerpoint presentation about an inventor from this era and his invention.

EXPLORATION: Invention Poster

Create a poster highlighting one of the important inventions of the Industrial Revolution. You may include how it changed life for people. Did it influence future inventions as well? How would your life today be different if it had never been invented? Include both the history of the invention and also the impacts. If your invention lends well to this, you might also include a 3-D component like a diorama or model to accompany your poster.

EXPLORATION: Luddites

If a machine is invented that can do the work of ten hand workers or artisans, then the economic benefits should be obvious. More can be produced for a much lower cost. If we're talking about cloth, then the cost per yard would go down and the demand will go up as people find they can afford not just one or two suits of clothes, but many. On the flip side, the machine just put ten skilled artisans out of business.

In the late 1700's and early 1800's there was a movement called the Luddites in Britain. They were skilled cloth weavers who made cloth on hand looms in their homes. With the advent of the big textile mills they found that they could no longer produce cloth cheaply enough to make a living at it. They lost their livelihoods and had to go to work in these mills, but for much lower wages. They wanted better wages and they wanted only skilled laborers who had completed training to be employed by the mills. So they decided the best way to handle their problems was to smash the new mechanical looms and, in some cases, beat or murder mill owners. It took the British government decades to completely quell the riots. Many of the Luddites were imprisoned and sent to Australia, and others were executed.

There is a wonderfully large chance that whatever work you begin doing in your adult life will disappear or become non-lucrative at some point.

Losing your job is bad, but it didn't happen to the Luddites overnight. If they were paying attention they would have seen it coming and prepared. You should pay attention to changes in technology, tax structures, demographics, and customer preferences. The Luddites couldn't hold back progress, and neither can you.

Brainstorm ways the Luddites could have dealt with their problems in a more constructive way. Choose one of the books you use on a regular basis in your education, like maybe your math book. Cover it with solid colored paper, like from a paper sack or butcher paper, then write all over the cover in colorful marker the things you'll do to make sure you can change with technology and not get stuck with awesomely useless skills. Paste a picture of the Luddites in the center, just to remind you of what happens to people who resist change instead of preparing for it.

😊 😊 😊 **EXPEDITION: Factory**
Find out if there's a factory near you that gives tours to families or school groups. We toured a candy factory and were amazed by the robots that helped make the candy. The Industrial Revolution changed everything from paper production to dairy processing to textile production, so any kind of factory will do. Once you schedule a tour learn more about the products and processes that the particular factory you'll be visiting uses so you can go armed with enough knowledge to understand what you're seeing and ask smart questions.

Additional Layer

Technology is still putting people out of business. Think of some modern day examples of a technology that has changed or destroyed an industry.

Actually, today that's happening at a much faster rate and affecting far more people than it did during the Industrial Revolution. That's why you need to learn to think and be adaptable, not just learn one skill set.

What would happen to you if you learned to be an auto mechanic and then technology changed so drastically that cars were completely different or no longer even needed? Think about it.

Famous Folks

Ned Ludd was a real person who, in a fit of rage, broke two weaving frames in about 1779. After that, any time a weaving frame was sabotaged it was blamed on "Ned Ludd," who by 1812 had become the mythical leader of the anti-industrialization movement.

Famous Folks

Lewis Hine was a sociologist and a photographer who traveled the United States and photographed people, especially children, working in factories, mines, and on farms. His photographs moved people to write labor laws regulating child labor.

☻ ☻ EXPLORATION: Child Labor

Since the beginning of time until the first part of the twentieth century children were economically essential to their families. In less developed countries children still are. Kids worked in the family business, which was farming more often than not, but also as weavers, cheese makers, bankers, sailors, and so on. Spending an entire childhood going to school was a luxury for only the ultra rich.

But after machines began to dominate economic life, child labor took on a whole new meaning. It was no longer a son working with his father or a daughter working with her mother. It was kids, sometimes as young as five, working six or eight hour days without a break, doing hard and dangerous labor down in a coal mine, in a textile factory, or in a smelter. Many factory owners liked to hire women and children because they could be paid less than men.

This little girl's job is to mend the broken threads on the spinning machine. She worked at a factory in Georgia, United States in 1909. The money she made was probably essential to her family's income. Public domain.

Look at the photos and captions from this page: http://www.historyplace.com/unitedstates/childlabor/.

Then read the primary source quotes from this page: http://www.historylearningsite.co.uk/children_industrial_revolution.htm.

Almost everything you find about the Industrial Revolution and especially about labor conditions and child labor will be negative. Reporters at the time and textbook writers today are trying to evoke an emotional response in you. Divide a sheet of paper into two columns. Make a list all the negative and all the positive things about child labor. You'll have to read between the lines and use logic to decide what about child labor was positive. The negative things should be easy to come up with.

😊 😊 EXPLORATION: Two Sides

Every story has two sides to it. Write two paragraphs. In the first one, imagine that you are a craftsman who has just been replaced by machinery. In the second paragraph pretend that you are a townsman who has access to many more products now that factories are dotting the nation. Everything is more readily available and cheaper now. See both sides.

Here are a few more:

Where you live, do you only go to Mom and Pop specialty stores, or do you do your shopping at larger stores? There are two sides to that.

Do you only buy American-made products, or do you buy imported ones? There are two sides to that too.

How are all these things related to each other and to the Industrial Revolution?

😊 😊 EXPLORATION: Capitalism

Capitalism means that individuals own and control property of all sorts and the government does not. Individuals choose where they will work, if they will open their own business, how they will run their business, and where they will spend their money. Individuals also bear the consequences of their own choices.

Economist Adam Smith

America and Britain both followed the capitalistic principles of Adam Smith, more or less, and it was this freedom, protection of private property, and hands-off government that had given rise to the incredible technological discoveries of the Industrial Era.

Unfortunately though, as Adam Smith recognized in 1776, if a businessman thinks he can get government to afford him special rules, grant him a monopoly, or regulate

One of the things that confuses people about Karl Marx versus the American Founders is that Marx was an optimist concerning human nature while the Founders were pessimists. The founders believed people were basically evil and therefore needed to be controlled or dissuaded from evil in some way, primarily through religion. Karl Marx had a lot of faith in human nature and thought people would just be nice and enlightened all on their own, so his system of economics and the governments that sprung from it had no way to control the behavior of the government or the governed except through a total breakdown and violence. It's one of life's little paradoxes.

Roller Coaster Tycoon is an excellent way to learn about capitalism. It's a video game where you build a theme park. You have to maximize profits, pay off loans, and keep customers happy. You can change prices, redesign rides, hire staff, and change entry fees.

his competition out of business, then **99%** of the time he will do just that. This practice of using the force of government to get a corner on the market is called "crony capitalism." We should just call it "cronyism" because there's nothing capitalist about it. It is, in fact, the very opposite of the free market.

There are certain conditions that must be met for a free market to work.

1. People must be virtuous.
2. Free trade between nations must exist.
3. Government must be small (large enough only to protect the rights of individuals, but not take care of them).
4. Currency must be stable.
5. People must be educated.

Capitalism is a necessary component of freedom and prosperity, but, like other freedoms, it is easily abused.

At the end of this unit you will find a "Capitalism and Cronyism" worksheet. Cut out the rectangles on the second sheet and match them to the rectangles on the first sheet. Glue the cut rectangles to the first sheet to create flaps that open, allowing you to read the definition or effects. The capitalism blocks are stacked neatly in a steady pyramid, but the cronyism blocks have fallen over and are a mess.

Capitalism and Cronyism

EXPLORATION: Robber Barons or Captains of Industry?

In medieval Germany the kings had very little power, and so their barons would become rulers unto themselves. Some of them went bad and used their power to terrorize the countryside, their neighbor barons, and any travelers unlucky enough to fall within their grasp. They stole and murdered because they could without any fear of the law.

Great industrial giants of the Industrial Revolution were compared to Robber Barons of the Middle Ages. People thought they must have amassed their wealth by underhanded means, by stealing, by taking unfair advantage, by abusing their employees, by fixing prices, or by bullying their competitors. So people used the force of government to punish these very successful and wealthy men. This is when the anti-trust laws came about in the United States.

A trust happens when several companies in the same industry collude to set prices or other standards in order to take advantage of consumers or labor. OPEC is a trust of oil producing nations around the world who collude to set prices. A monopoly is when one company owns all of a particular industry, like if one company owned all the chicken production in the entire nation, they could set the price and if you wanted chicken you would have to pay their price. Additionally, if you were a chicken farmer, then you would have to work for them. Trusts and monopolies are the opposite of capitalism, though many people think they happen because of capitalism.

Compare the Central Pacific Railroad and the Union Pacific Railroad, both of which were granted special treatment and subsidies by government, to the Great Northern Railway of James J. Hill, who remained independent of government. This site does a great job of explaining the history and differences between the railroads: http://www.sjsu.edu/faculty/watkins/hill.htm.

While you are reading the website to your kids and teaching them about this concept, have them work on a train craft. Cut a train shape out of card stock or construction paper. Cut a toilet paper roll in half and cut a slit in each half. Stick your train shape into the slits on the top of the toilet paper rolls to form wheels. Paste a photo of James J. Hill on one engine. Paste a photo of Thomas Clark Durant, the man who controlled the railroad in its early days and bribed congress to give special favors to the railway, to another train.

On the Web

If you want to expand on the lesson about capitalism with your high schooler, check out this set of lesson plans that could cover several weeks: http://www.fte.org/teacher-resources/lesson-plans/is-capitalism-good-for-the-poor/.

On the Web

This short video about the making of a pencil explains how the "invisible hand" in the free market works.

https://www.youtube.com/watch?v=IY-O3tOqDISE

It is based on the book, *I, Pencil* by Leonard E. Read.

Memorization Station

Memorize the definitions to these words:

Robber Baron

Captain of Industry

Trust

Industrial Revolution

Capitalism

Monopoly

Luddites

Trust-busting

Unions

Direct Action

GEOGRAPHY: U.S. LANDSCAPES

Famous Folks

Laura Ingalls Wilder was a pioneer girl who wrote children's stories based on her childhood living in the northern woods and then on the Great Plains of America. Her stories are beloved children's literature and an interesting look at how the geography of America shaped its history.

Explanation

This unit focuses on the natural landscape and how the natural landscape of America has influenced the nation and its people.

In Unit 4-9 we'll get into the economics of the United States and then in 4-11 we'll talk about man-made landmarks.

Salt Dough Recipe

This recipe is enough for two 16" x 12" maps.

4 cups flour
2 cups salt
2 Tbsp. cream of tartar
2 cups water

Mix the flour, salt, and cream of tartar, then add the water, stirring and kneading until smooth. It should end up the consistency of play dough.

The United States is one of the largest countries in the world in terms of land area. It's also situated in the middle latitudes so that the climate ranges from cold continental with howling cold winters and blazing hot summers to sub-tropical with year round heat. The United States also stretches from one ocean, the Atlantic, clear across the continent to the other ocean, the Pacific. In between there are coastal, mountain, forest, plain, swamp, desert, and river environments. It is one of the most varied and beautiful countries on the planet.

The varied landscapes and abundant natural resources have contributed to the prosperity and happiness of the American people. Timber, irrigation, farmland, mineral resources, oil, coal, recreation, and beauty are all abundant in this land. Americans are very conscious of their natural heritage and work hard to preserve and use their resources wisely.

😊 😊 😊 **EXPLORATION: Relief Map**

Make a relief map of the contiguous United States. Use salt dough and a map of the United States for reference. Form the outline of the United States on top of a large stiff piece of cardboard, pinch the dough into mountains, making the Rockies larger than the Appalachians and so forth. Allow the dough to dry, then paint the mountains brown, the highlands orange, and the low lying land green. After the paint has dried, paint on the rivers and lakes. Once all that paint is dry, use a permanent marker to label the mountain ranges, rivers, plains, coastal features and so on. Draw on the coastlines of Canada and Mexico, then paint the oceans blue, leaving the neighboring countries unpainted.

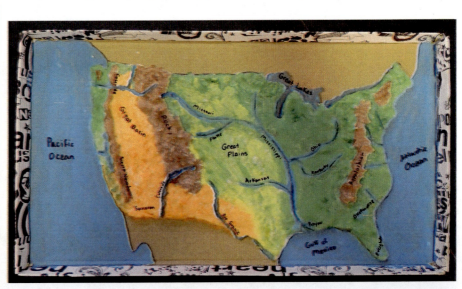

Here is a list of features you may want to include (older kids can make a more detailed map than younger kids).

Mountains
Rocky
Appalachian
Cascade Range
Sierra Nevada

Wetlands
Okefenokee Swamp
Everglades Swamp
Mississippi River Delta

Grasslands
Great Plains

Rivers
Mississippi
Missouri
Ohio
Hudson
Rio Grande
Savannah
St. Lawrence
Columbia
San Joaquin
Colorado
Snake

Deserts
Sonoran
Mojave
Great Basin
Chihuahuan

Lakes
Great Lakes
Great Salt Lake
Salton Sea

On the Web
This five minute video, set to "America the Beautiful" shows images of beautiful places in each of the fifty states: https://www.youtube.com/watch?v=yDmmRj-mosEs.

It makes a great introduction to this unit.

EXPLORATION: Rivers of the United States
The United States has many rivers. These rivers are used for recreation, power production, transportation, irrigation, as a drinking water supply, and for wildlife. The largest river system in the United States is the Mississippi and the hundreds of rivers and streams that are tributaries to it. Many major cities of the United States are located along rivers.

At the end of this unit, you'll find a map of the rivers of the United States. The state borders are shown as well. Trace over the rivers in blue and label them. The names of the rivers to label are on the map. Use a student atlas to find the answers.

Writer's Workshop
Choose a particular geographic location and use it as the setting of a story. You could have space aliens invade the Okefenokee Swamp, with the Swampers speaking Elizabethan style English to them. Or you could have foreign agents destroy a dam and create the Salton Sea. You get the idea.

Additional Layer
Most waterways in the United States are publicly owned. Even if a river or stream runs right through your property, you don't actually own the water. Anyone can use that water for activities that aren't harmful to others. For example, you can go boating down the river, but you can't dump your garbage in it because dumping your garbage would harm other people and the wildlife.

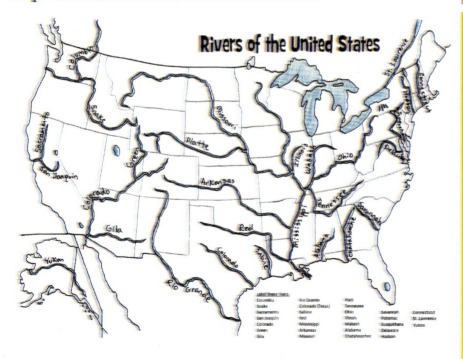

Rivers of the United States

Label these rivers:
Columbia
Snake
Sacramento
San Joaquin
Colorado
Green
Gila
Rio Grande
Colorado (Texas)
Sabine
Red
Mississippi
Arkansas
Missouri
Platt
Tennessee
Ohio
Illinois
Wabash
Alabama
Chatahoochee
Savannah
Potomac
Susquehana
Delaware
Hudson
Connecticut
St. Lawrence
Yukon

Additional Layer

President Lyndon Johnson signed the Wild and Scenic Rivers Act in 1968. The Act preserves some of the rivers of the United States in their pristine condition, undammed, unpolluted, and undeveloped. You can find out more here: http://www.rivers.gov/. Be sure to look at the "kids" part of the site.

This page has some games about the wild and scenic rivers in the U.S.: http://www.rivers.gov/kids/games.html.

On the Web

This quick online game helps kids identify and learn the major rivers around the United States: http://www.softschools.com/social_studies/geography/rivers_of_the_united_states/.

Fabulous Fact

Geologists think the Appalachians were once as tall as the Rockies. But the Appalachians are much older and they have eroded down to the present rounded size.

☺ ☻ EXPLORATION: Mountain Ranges

The United States has two major mountain ranges and many smaller ones. The two big mountain ranges run up either side of the continent, the Rockies in the west and the much older Appalachians in the east. These mountain ranges provided barriers to early settlers and kept the major cities mostly along the two coast lines. Mountains are used for mining and recreation and most major National Parks are in mountainous regions.

There is a map of mountain ranges to color and paste at the end of this unit. First, color the mountain ranges in brown. Then color the water on the map blue. Color the United States light green. Color Mexico and Canada dark green. Now cut off the right hand side of the page along the light gray line. Cut out each of the mountain ranges along the dotted lines. Next give the kids clues about the mountains and the kids determine which mountain range you're describing. When they get it right, have them glue the mountains on in the right places. There is a completed map below to use for reference.

And here are the clues:

1. This mountain range is the wettest spot in the lower 48 states, supporting a temperate rain forest on its western flank. The mountains form a cluster of mountain peaks covered with evergreen forested slopes. These are fold mountains formed from the upheaval of the oceanic and continental crust along the margin of the North American plate. They were named for the home of the Greek gods because of their beauty. (Olympic)

2. These mountains are the most rugged portion of their range. Many of the peaks in the range are named after presidents, including Mount Washington, which recorded the highest wind

speed of any place in North America. The mountains are also criss-crossed with trails and huts for hikers to use. They're located in Vermont, New Hampshire, and Maine. (Green and White Mountains)

3. This is a small isolated group of low mountains in the middle of the great plains. They have been the site of battles between Native tribes and American soldiers, gold rushes, and the famous Mt. Rushmore carving of the presidents. (Black Hills)

4. These mountains are fold mountains formed when the Pacific Plate slid underneath the North American Plate. They are made of continental granite and are rich in mining resources. Within this large mountain range there are dozens of smaller sub-ranges. This is the largest mountain range in North America. (Rocky Mountains)

5. These uplift mountains block most precipitation from reaching Nevada and Utah. The famous Lake Tahoe is located high amid these peaks as are the biggest trees in the world, the Giant Sequoia. The name of these mountains is Spanish for snowy mountains. (Sierra Nevada Range)

6. This range is divided into two parts, a north and a south, by the San Francisco Bay area. These mountains were the site of the most famous gold rush in history. (Coast Range)

7. This area is a huge uplifted dome, eroded and dissected by rivers, a formation known as a dissected plateau. It is made mostly of limestone and has many cave systems running through it. These mountains are an isolated high land area in between the Great Plains and the Southern coastal plain. (Ozarks)

8. These mountains used to be as high and rugged as the Rockies in the west, but they are much, much older and have eroded into soft low forms. Their slopes are covered with mixed forests of evergreen and deciduous birch, beech, pine, fir, maple, hemlock, and others. Within this main range are many sub-ranges. (Appalachians)

9. These mountains are volcanic and active today. They are high mountains, covered in snow throughout the year. They block the moisture from the sea reaching inland, creating severe rain shadows. The most famous peaks in this range are Mt. St. Helens, Mt. Rainier, and Mt. Baker. The abundance of water and fast moving rivers coming off the slopes has generated a great deal of hydroelectric power, which is used all over the Western United States. (Cascade Range)

Additional Layer

Mount Rushmore is a carving of four U.S. presidents into a granite wall of the Black Hills in South Dakota.

The project's purpose was to create a tourism demand to boost the economy of the area. It worked. About 2 million people visit Mt. Rushmore every year.

Think up a project of national importance that could bring tourism to your town. What would you build? Write a report about it as though it already exists.

Fabulous Facts

The Ozark Mountains are actually a high, uplifted dome of rock that has been dissected by erosion into distinct mountains. Many millions of years ago this area was an island in the Paleozoic sea. Reef formations and sandstone from that sea can still be found in this area. Underlying all are ancient layers of granite and basalt.

Additional Layer

Beaches are another important landscape in the United States. The more southerly coastal states have beautiful sandy beaches that millions of people visit every year for recreation.

Besides recreation, these beaches and coastal waters are home to species such as sand crabs, clams, snails, sand dollars, mites, gulls, herons, beach grass, and animals like the sea turtle that use the beach for nesting.

Do some research into the animals that live on the beach, and on your next visit look for some of them.

Additional Layer

Caves are another fascinating American landscape. Mammoth Caves in Kentucky are probably the most famous in the U.S., but there's a good chance there's a cave system in your neighborhood to go explore.

☺ ☺ ☺ EXPLORATION: The Appalachian Trail

At approximately 2,200 miles, the Appalachian Trail stretches from Maine to Georgia. It traverses the length of the Appalachian Range and passes over mountains, through valleys, and across streams and rivers. Most of the trail is in the wilderness, but it also passes through towns.

Thousands of species of animals and plants live in the region surrounding the Appalachian Trail. Some of the better known animals include the black bear, timber rattle snake, copperhead snake, deer, elk, moose, and of course, mosquitoes and black flies. The plants in this region include oak and tulip trees in the south and maple and birch in the north with conifers in the far north.

At the end of this unit you will find a printable map of the Appalachian Trail. Print this onto card stock. The map pages must be joined top to bottom with tape to make one long map. You can look up information online to find details and images to add to the map.

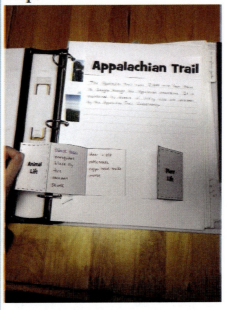

You will also find some Appalachian Trail notebooking printables to add to your map pages. The top page of the map can fold down over the bottom page to make a cover. There is a title strip and foldable booklets to print and cut out to add to this cover. You will also have room to add some basic information about the Appalachian Trail such as where it runs, how far, and the history of its creation.

☺ ☺ ☺ EXPLORATION: Swamps

A swamp is a forested wetland. Some of the best known swamps in the United States include the Everglades in Florida, the Okefenokee Swamp in Florida and Georgia, and the Bayous of Louisiana. Find each of these places on a map of the United States. Then read a book about swamps. We like *Marshes and Swamps* by Gail Gibbons or *One Small Square: Swamp* by Donald Silver for the youngest students. *America's Wetlands: Guide to Plants and Animals* by Marianne Wallace is perfect for middle grades students or even high schoolers who want a quick overview.

Then make a miniature diorama depicting a swamp scene. You will need one sheet of card stock or construction paper, construction paper in brown and green, markers, crayons, and/or colored pencils, glue, and scissors.

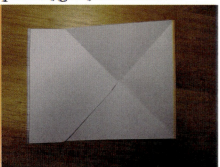 

1. Fold the sheet of card stock or construction paper on the diagonal in two directions so that one end of the paper is divided evenly into fourths on the diagonal.

2. Cut along one of the diagonal folds, beginning at the side of paper, not at the corner. Tuck the cut edge under the longer

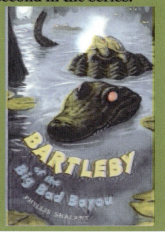

Fabulous Fact

Parts of the desert landscape include fantastic rock formations. Many of the rocks in the desert are sandstone. Sandstone is pretty soft and is easily eroded by wind and flash floods into fascinating shapes like these hoodoos from Bryce Canyon, Utah.

Teaching Tip

Most of the projects in this section can be applied to any landscape, so if you want to focus on some other region of U.S. landscapes, feel free to adapt the projects.

Additional Layer

Forestland, especially in the west, is often federally or state owned land. The forests are used for recreational activities like hiking, camping, hunting, horseback riding, and ATVs. Forests are also managed to produce timber and run mining operations.

Find the forested areas of the U.S. on a map.

flat piece so that you end up with a triangle standing above the flat edge. This way you can see how the background will be positioned.

3. Decorate the background on this sheet of paper using the crayons and markers.

4. Cut out trees and other decorations from the colored construction paper. Glue them to the background sheet.

5. Finish up by adding short reports or fact sheets about American swamps to the back of the diorama.

😀 😊 EXPLORATION: Southwest Deserts

A desert is a place that receives less than 10 inches of rain a year. The deserts of the United States are created from coastal mountain ranges that block the rain. They are all located in the Western United States. The three largest deserts in the United States are the Chihuahuan, the Sonoran, and the Mojave. There are other cold weather deserts in the Great Basin and the Colombia and Snake River Basins.

Read a book about deserts. We like *Desert Giant* by Barbara Bash for kids up to 6th grade. *One Day in the Desert* by Jean Craighead George is great for middle grades. Older teens can research information online, especially focusing on one of the three largest deserts.

Follow up your research by making a desert field guide. Start by printing the cover from the end of this unit onto card stock. The cover includes a map of the deserts of the United States. Then on inside pages put facts you learned about the desert. Include pop-ups, flaps to open, and pockets for more interest.

☺ ☺ ☺ EXPLORATION: West Coast

The northwest coast of the United States is very rocky and rugged. Tide pools, which serve as homes to many animals, are formed along the rocky coast. The rocks are shaped by the pounding sea into caves, stacks, and arches. This area is actively changing with frequent earthquakes, occasional volcanic activity, and powerful wave erosion. It is also wet, and the temperatures remain cooler in the summer and warmer in the winter than regions just a little further inland because of the influence of the ocean. The combination of temperate weather and lots of water makes this area lush and green with some areas even reaching rain forest status.

Look up some images of the "Oregon Coast" or "Washington Coast" online. Find this area on a map of the United States.

Then make a coast in a jar scene. Use a quart-sized plastic or glass jar. Old peanut butter jars or canning jars work great. Find some pebbles in various sizes outside. Clean and dry the pebbles, then paint some sea creatures onto your rocks using acrylic paints.

Mix up a little plaster of Paris according to package directions. Placing the jar on its side, pour and spoon plaster of Paris across the inside side of the jar (now the bottom, with the jar tipped on its side). Place the pebbles you found into the wet plaster. Sprinkle some sand between the rocks. Let it all dry. Wash out the excess sand. Then add a little water and screw the lid on tightly. Color

---

Additional Layer

The United States includes over 18,000 named islands. Some of the more well known island locations include the Hawaiian Islands, Florida Keys, Channel Islands in California, and the San Juan Islands in Washington State.

How is an island landscape unique? What differences are there between a freshwater island and a saltwater island?

This is Deer Isle, Maine.

Choose an island in the United States and learn about the people, animals, and plants that inhabit the island.

Fabulous Fact

The coast of New England is also rocky and rugged, not to mention beautiful.

Teaching Tip

Nearly every project you do should be accompanied by outside reading and at least a bit of writing. Using these skills for learning is the point.

Additional Layer

In the early days of America the land seemed so vast and the natural resources so abundant that they were used without reservation. But losing the entire population of carrier pigeons, nearly destroying the buffalo species, and facing hunger because of the Dust Bowl drove some hard lessons home for Americans.

The conservation movement began in the late 1800's and built up in the early 1900's into a set of practices that allows the use of natural resources without destroying them.

Using natural resources isn't wrong, but using them responsibly is essential in order to have them for the future.

Today only small patches of virgin (never been farmed) prairies still exist in the United States. Learn more about these prairie preserves and how they are important.

Additional Layer

Find out what the economy of the plains states is based on. Does the economy have anything to do with the geography of this region?

a mountain scene on a piece of paper and tape it to the outside of the jar so that it backs the ocean scene when viewed from the side.

☺ ☺ ☺ EXPLORATION: Great Plains

The central part of the United States is shielded so that it gets less rainfall than the coastal areas, but it is not so dry as the western deserts. This area is a prairie full of grasses, wildflowers, bushes, jackrabbits, gophers, snakes, bugs of all sorts, deer, and buffalo. The land is mostly flat and spreads between major mountain ranges to the east and west. These geographical features mean that the summers are hot and dry and full of storms and the winters are bitterly cold, windy, and snowy.

Watch this video of the wildlife of the Great Plains: https://www.youtube.com/watch?v=pQKwzhEXLEo. Find the Great Plains on a map of the United States.

To help in understanding the diversity of life on the plains, make a Great Plains pop-up scene.

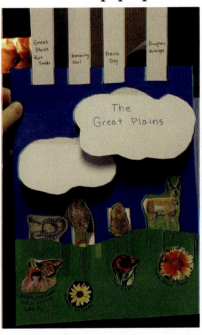 

1. Find pictures of animals and plants of the Great Plains online. We used four plants and four animals. Print them onto card stock in a small size. Cut the animals and plants out.

2. Cut a piece of green card stock so it is about a third of a normal sheet of paper. We cut ours with a wavy line to represent hills. Then cut slits all down the top edge of the green paper to represent grass.

3. Glue your pictures of plants to the green grass card stock piece. Label each plant. We just used common names.

4. Cut four strips of card stock, one inch wide and the length of the sheet of paper. Glue your animals to the bottom of these strips.

5. Using a utility knife, cut slits just over an inch wide for the animal strips to fit through in a piece of blue card stock. One slit should be about an inch above the top edge of your grass paper as it is positioned at the bottom. The other slit should be near the top edge of the blue background paper.

6. Thread the animal strips through the slits from the bottom of the page, down first, then up through the slits near the top of the page.

7. Glue the green grass to the blue background along the very outside edges of the paper, bottom and sides. The grass will form a pocket that the animals can hide behind until you pull up on their tabs to reveal them.

8. At the top of the tabs write the name of each animal. We wrote ours so it was hidden until the tab was pulled up.

9. Finally, add a couple of clouds to the scene and glue them down along the top edge of the cloud so they too can become flaps. Under the flaps write some facts about the Great Plains.

😊 😊 😊 EXPLORATION: The Great Lakes

The Great Lakes are five interconnected fresh water lakes in the north central part of the United States. They are connected to the sea via the St. Lawrence River, and ocean-going vessels ply their waters. Man-made canals have also connected the lakes to the Hudson River and the Mississippi water course. The lakes are extremely useful for transportation, so large cities like Chicago, Toledo, and Detroit have grown up on their shores.

The lake region has hot summers and cold winters. The lakes also contribute in the winter to extra snowfall because of the evaporation of water from their surface. This is called lake-effect snow.

Watch this video about the Great Lakes: https://www.youtube.com/watch?v=sHjwfneXRsU.

Freehand draw a map of the Great Lakes. Label each lake and add pictures to the map showing what the region looks like. You could include cities, boats, fish, trees, animals, and birds. You can either draw your pictures or find images from the Internet to print and paste on.

Additional Layer

While the Great Plains are crossed by many rivers, the area is very dry, too dry for crops to grow well. So farmers must irrigate. One of the primary sources of irrigation is a massive underground water reservoir called the Ogallala Aquifer. Learn more about the aquifer and what is good and bad about using it.

Famous Folks

The Plains Indians were nomadic people who lived on the Great Plains and followed the buffalo herds for food. They lived in tipis, rode horses, and fought bitterly against the encroachment of white settlers, thus earning a reputation as the iconic North American Indian across the world. Find out more about a specific tribe and what life was like within the Great Plains then.

Fabulous Fact

Ice fishing is super popular in the Great Lakes region. Learn more.

SCIENCE: ENERGY

Potential Energy and Kinetic Energy

Watch this video of dominoes falling to see how a little bit of kinetic energy can release a whole lot of potential energy . . . it just takes a little push. http://www.youtube.com/watch?v=y97rBdSYbkg

Famous Folks

James Prescott Joule was an English scientist who, from childhood, was fascinated with electricity. He used to give the servants and his family members electrical shocks just to see what would happen. He discovered the connection between heat and mechanical work, blasting the caloric heat theory to smithereens.

The joule unit to measure work is named in his honor.

Work and energy are technical terms to a physicist. Work is done when force is used to move an object. Energy is the ability to do work. When work is done energy is converted from one form to another. There are four types of energy: potential, kinetic, chemical, and electrical.

Potential energy is stored energy. The energy waiting to be released when the mouse springs the trap is potential energy. The energy waiting to be released as you let the car go down the ramp is potential energy. If you are standing up on top of a box, you have potential energy as you jump off. A sling shot pulled fully back has potential energy.

Kinetic energy is active moving energy. It is the energy that is being used up as the mouse trap snaps shut, the car rolls down the ramp or you fall to the floor from the box. And as you let the sling shot go, the kinetic energy of the moving band shoots a rock out.

Chemical energy is another type of stored energy. Chemical energy is stored in the bonds of chemicals like protein or carbohydrates that you eat. Batteries also use chemical energy to store energy in bonds.

Electrical energy is electricity, or moving electrons. It can be converted into light, sound, or movement to power machines like washers, vacuums, televisions, computers, and more.

☺ ☺ ☺ EXPLORATION: Joules

Work was first used as a technical physics term by Gaspard-Gustave Coriolis, a French mathematician, who was figuring out how much energy it would take to lift a bucket of water out of a coal mine in 1826 using the new steam engines of the day. Since calculating work required a new unit of measure (inches, pounds, meters, and Celsius are all different sorts of units of measure) the unit "joule" was assigned to represent one unit of work. Joule is named after the English physicist James Prescott Joule.

The mathematical definition of a joule is:

$$J = \frac{Kg \cdot m^2}{s^2}$$

J stands for joules, kg stands for kilograms, m stands for meters, and s stands for seconds. The equation means that a joule is one kilogram of weight lifted one meter, divided by the force of gravity, which is roughly 9.8 on earth. To find an object that is worth 1 unit of weight for this equation, you divide one by the force of gravity and you get .101936 kg.

To visualize what one joule represents find an object that is about

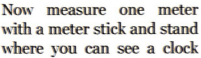

.101936 kg in weight. You can round the weight to approximately 100 g. We found a partially used tube of toothpaste, a small apple, a cordless mouse, and a box of gelatin dessert that were all close (enough) to 100 g.

Now measure one meter with a meter stick and stand where you can see a clock

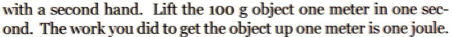

with a second hand. Lift the 100 g object one meter in one second. The work you did to get the object up one meter is one joule.

Fabulous Fact

Joules are hard to wrap your brain around because normally the things we measure have one dimension like the length of a line or the time it takes to do something, but joules is three dimensional: distance, mass, and time all measured simultaneously.

Memorization Station

Energy is a property of matter that can be transferred from one object to another or converted into other forms, but cannot be created or destroyed.

Fabulous Fact

Energy is difficult to define because it can exist in so many different forms.

Here are some of the forms energy can take:

Potential energy

Kinetic energy

Chemical energy

Elastic energy

Nuclear energy

Thermal energy

Radiant energy

Electromagnetic energy

Each of these forms can be converted into another and each behaves differently.

Fabulous Fact

According to the mass-energy equivalence theory, energy and mass are closely related. Energy can be converted to mass and mass can be converted to energy. In fact, any time you add energy to an object it gains in mass. If you had a sensitive enough instrument you could measure the gain in mass that happens when you heat something.

Additional Layer

Energy is a component of virtually everything. The planets stay in orbit because of energy. The water cycle happens because of energy. Living things stay alive and reproduce because of energy. Your trip to the store to buy your stuff relied on energy from harvesting natural resources to manufacturing and transporting goods to fueling your vehicle or body to get to the store.

People often talk about energy in terms of fueling modern society. Where does the energy come from for that fuel? If the primary fuel sources were cut off, what would happen? How important is it to make sure reliable sources of energy exist?

What if you did the lifting more slowly but still went 1 meter and still lifted 1 kg? Would it still take one joule?

Yes, because the seconds in this problem represent acceleration, not speed. So if I lift the jar more slowly then my work is spread across more time, which means I just do less work per second, but not less work overall.

Joules are also used as a unit of energy when people calculate for electricity. It really means the same thing - how much effort does it take to move something a certain distance?

☻ EXPLORATION: Calculate Joules

To calculate the amount of joules needed to heat an object you'll need:

- Thermometer
- Water in a pot
- Calculator
- Timer or stopwatch
- Scale
- Graph paper

1. Weigh your pan empty. Record the weight in grams.
2. Fill the pan ¼ full of tap water and weigh again in grams. Record the weight. Subtract the weight of the pan to get the weight of the water in grams.
3. Take the temperature of the water with a Celsius thermometer.
4. Heat the water for one minute and take the temperature.
5. Keep heating the water for four more minutes (five minutes total), taking the temperature every minute. Record your data in a table that looks like this:

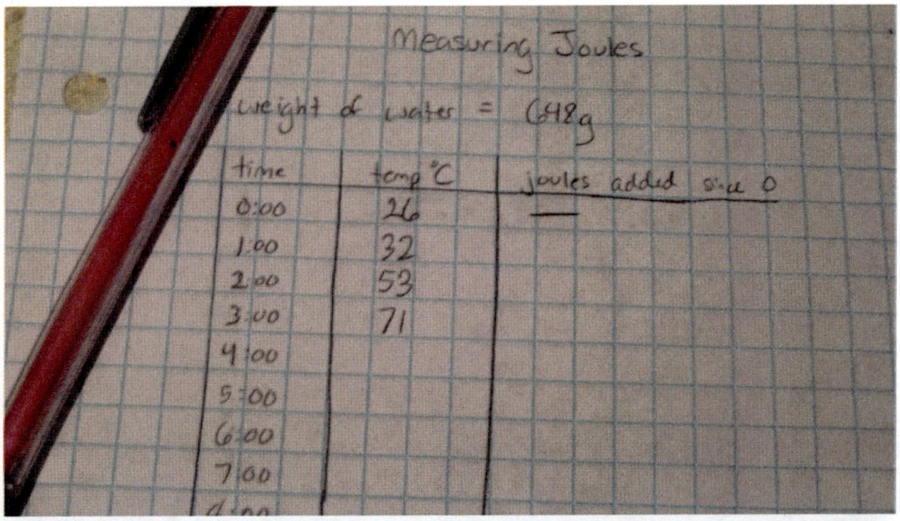

6. Subtract the temperature after one minute from the beginning temperature.

7. Multiply by the specific heat capacity of liquid water, which is 4.1813.

8. Multiply by the weight of the water in grams. The answer is the number of joules that entered the water during heating.

9. Repeat your calculations for each temperature reading. Create a graph and a table to show your data.

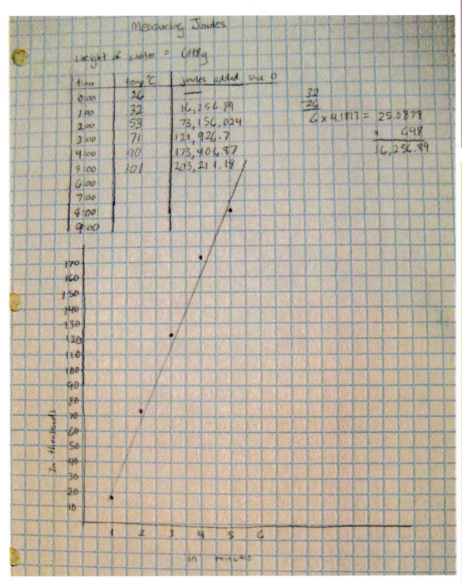

Additional Layer

Heat capacity is the amount of heat that a particular substance requires to be added to it to raise the temperature one degree Celsius. Every type of matter has a unique heat capacity. Water has one of the highest heat capacities of any known substance. This allows water, which is present in vast quantities on earth, to moderate the climate of the whole planet.

Famous Folks

Thomas Young was a polymath, which means he was an expert in diverse branches which included musical theory, medicine, physics, foreign languages, and Egyptology (he helped translate the Rosetta Stone). He was also the first scientist to use the term "energy" in the modern scientific sense.

☻ EXPLORATION: Intro To Work and Energy

Watch the excellent Khan Academy videos about work and energy: http://www.khanacademy.org/science/physics/mechanics/v/introduction-to-work-and-energy.

Practice with the work-energy equation which is:

$$\text{Force} = \tfrac{1}{2}(\text{mass})(\text{velocity})^2$$

The equation means that the amount of force applied to an object, (for example, the amount of force to lift an apple) is equal to the kinetic energy of the object. For an apple siting on the table the kinetic energy would be zero and the force would be zero because the apple is not moving. That's quite different from an apple being thrown twenty feet in the air.

☺ ☻ EXPLORATION: Gravity

Everywhere on earth the force with which gravity pulls on objects is about the same amount:

$$9.80 \; \frac{\text{m/sec}}{\text{sec}}$$

You see, gravity is really a function of acceleration and not speed. If I drop an object it isn't immediately at its fastest; it accelerates as it falls and gravity tells us how quickly it accelerates. So what the above number for gravity (nine point eight zero meters per second per second) means is that the ball I just dropped is moving at 9.80 meters per second in the first second, but in the second second it is moving twice as fast and in the third three times as fast and in the fourth four times as fast and so on.

The equation to determine how fast a free-falling object is moving at any given point is:

$$v = g \cdot t$$

V stands for velocity, g is the gravity constant, and t is the time in seconds. Notice that it does not matter how much mass the falling object has.

Now do some calculations to determine how fast something is falling if you drop it off the top of a cliff. Imagine it takes ten seconds for the rock to hit the bottom. That means you will need ten calculations. Graph your calculations.

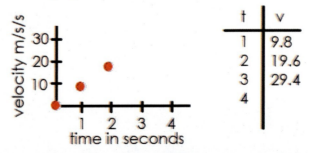

t	v
1	9.8
2	19.6
3	29.4
4	

Can you figure out how long it will take your rock to hit the ground if you drop it off a hundred meter high cliff? Calculate the time it will take for an object to fall off a real cliff. Search for the height of a real cliff (or the height of a tall building or bridge) and calculate the time it will take for the object to fall.

☻ EXPLORATION: Potential Energy

Potential energy is the energy that something has before the energy is released. If I hold a raw egg above the floor, the egg has potential energy. As the egg falls to the floor, the potential energy decreases as the kinetic energy (energy of motion) increases. Finally, when the egg hits the floor, the energy is used up in vibrations that make sound, in waves that are passed through the floor and ultimately into the earth, and in flinging the bits of egg across my formerly clean kitchen tile.

We can calculate exactly how much potential energy that egg has by measuring the height of the egg above the floor in meters and multiplying the height by the weight in kilograms and the force of gravity, which on earth is 9.8. Here's the equation for measuring potential energy.

$$U = mgh$$

Potential Energy = weight(kg) x gravity(9.8) x height (m)

Gather some objects and calculate their potential energy. The unit for potential energy is joules, as long as you use kilograms, and meters for the units in the equation above. What happens to potential energy if the weight of the objects varies? What about if the height you drop them from changes?

☻ EXPLORATION: Kinetic Energy

Kinetic energy is the energy of motion. In the falling egg example above, we see that as it falls it loses potential energy and gains kinetic energy. That means that the moment before it hits the floor the egg has maxed out its kinetic energy and used up all of its potential energy.

If you wrote down the potential energies of the objects you dropped in the last exploration, you can calculate how fast your stuff was moving as you dropped it since the kinetic energy will equal the potential energy. Here's the equation:

$$E_K = \tfrac{1}{2}mv^2$$

Additional Layer

There are four fundamental interactions between energy in the universe. These are gravity, strong, weak, and electromagnetic. Gravity is the weakest of all these forces. The strong and weak forces are in the nuclei of atoms. And electromagnetic forces have to do with charges in particles.

To understand the four fundamental forces of physics, which you should do if you are in high school or older, watch this series of videos: https://www.youtube.com/watch?v=Yv3EMq2Dgq-8&list=PLsNB4peY-6C6JDc1HcVKjjYzVB-oBYEXexd.

Memorization Station

Potential energy is stored energy.

Kinetic energy is the energy of motion.

On the Web

This video from Mr. Andersen explains kinetic and potential energy:

https://www.youtube.com/watch?v=BSWl_Zj-CZs.

Famous Folks

Gaspard-Gustav de Coriolis was the French engineer and scientist who first defined kinetic energy and its relationship to work.

He applied his calculations to rotating systems. The atmospheric rotations of the earth were named after him, the Coriolis Effect.

Fabulous Fact

The Chocolate Chip launcher uses a special type of potential energy called elastic energy. Elastic energy is employed any time a substance is compressed or stretched out of its normal shape and upon release returns to its normal shape. A coiled spring is an example of elastic energy.

So there are several types of potential energy: gravitational, elastic, and chemical.

E_k is Kinetic energy, m is the mass (in kilograms), and v is the velocity in meters per second.

If my egg had a potential energy of .882 joules, then at the moment before my egg hit the floor it also had a kinetic energy of .882 joules. My egg was 1.5 meters above the floor and weighed .056 kilograms. I can set up my equation like this:

$$.882 = \frac{1}{2}(.056v^2)$$

Multiply both sides of the equation by 2 to get rid of the 1/2.

$$1.76 = .056v^2$$

Divide by .056 on both sides of the equation.

$$31.5 = v^2$$

Take the square root of both sides.

$$5.61 \text{ mps} = v$$

Try calculating the speed of your falling stuff.

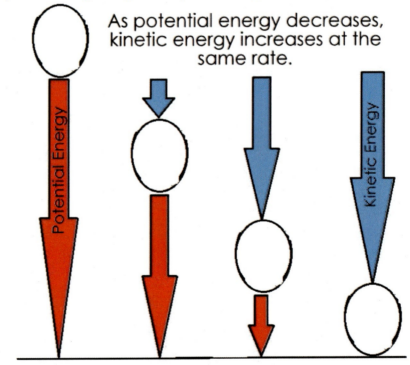

As potential energy decreases, kinetic energy increases at the same rate.

☺ ☻ EXPLORATION: Chocolate Chip Launcher

Potential energy is the energy stored in an object. In other words, if I am up high on a ladder I might fall. Falling takes energy, like all motion. I have stored that energy in my body by climbing the ladder. Any object that could potentially fall, roll, slide downward, or be ejected vertically or horizontally has potential energy stored.

If I do fall, my potential energy is transferred into kinetic energy, the energy of motion, as I fall. At the moment I hit the ground the potential energy has all been transferred into kinetic energy.

Potential energy can be stored elastically, like when a bowstring is pulled back or when a chocolate chip is launched from a stretched balloon.

You need:

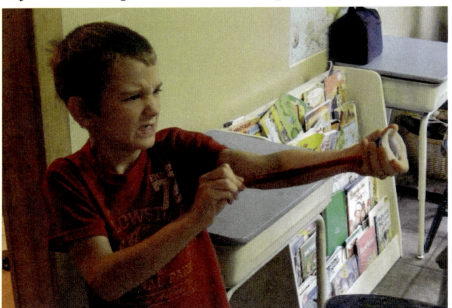

- Balloon
- Plastic bottle with threaded lid
- Chocolate chips

1. Cut off the mouth of the bottle

2. Cut a hole in the lid, leaving just a ring (try using a knife)

3. Stretch the lip of the balloon over the rim of the bottle mouth, then screw the lid on over the balloon so that the balloon is pinched between the bottle and the lid.

4. Put a chocolate chip inside the balloon.

5. Grasp the rim with one hand and pull back on the balloon with the other.

6. Let it go! You might want to launch this outside as your chocolate chip can fly about sixty feet. (We're not responsible for injuries or damage due to chocolate chip collisions or ricochets.)

Teaching Tip

Younger kids should understand that it takes energy to do work. They should also understand the difference between potential energy and kinetic energy and that joules is the measurement of energy.

In addition, older teens should understand the gravity constant, the equations for potential and kinetic energy, and the equation for energy in a pendulum.

If you are struggling with these concepts we highly recommend videos, many referenced in the sidebars.

On the Web

Here's a short video that shows the effect of elastic potential energy on a watermelon. It's fun.

https://www.youtube.com/watch?v=kr13B-7zptWc

Fabulous Fact

The word "energy" comes from the Greek word *energeia*, which means operation or activity.

When you pulled back on the balloon, stretching it, the balloon has a whole lot of potential energy. When you let go of the balloon, the energy is changed into kinetic energy and that energy is transferred to your chocolate chip which flies like a bird until it is slowed by friction from the air and pulled to earth with gravity.

😊 😊 😊 **EXPEDITION: Sledding**

Find a sledding hill near you and explain potential and kinetic energy before you slide.

The top of the hill. Anticipation. The ride down. Stimulation and trepidation. The bottom of the hill. Satisfaction.

These three stages - the top, the ride down, and the bottom - are examples of energy in action. At the top you have potential energy; you have energy stored just by being in a high place from which you can fall or slide down. If you didn't have stored energy your sled would just sit there; you would never fall down the hill. Instead you would have to push all the way down, no matter how slick or steep the hill. While you are sliding down the hill you still have potential energy during the rest of your ride, but that potential energy is getting less and less as you approach the bottom of the hill. You are gaining more and more kinetic energy as you approach the bottom of the hill. Kinetic energy is the energy of motion. When you get to the bottom of the hill, your kinetic energy is maxed out and your potential energy is gone.

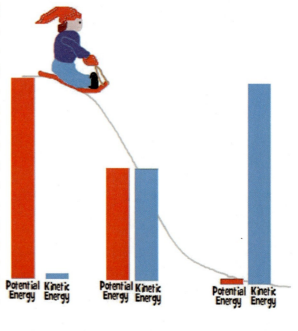

Energy never disappears, but is changed from one form to another, so where does all that kinetic energy go that you have at the bottom of the hill? Most of it goes to heat and sound. To make the swooshing sound of your sled sliding over the snow requires energy. And though there's not much heat, the friction of your sled against the snow does produce heat, enough to slow your sled at the bottom of the hill. (We'll talk more about conservation of energy in Unit 4-5).

☻ ☻ EXPLORATION: Energy in a Pendulum

Way back in Unit 1-9 we put a kid on a swing and timed the oscillation speed of the swinger.

You should have discovered that it didn't matter how high the swinger was swinging, the swinger took exactly the same amount of time to swing through one oscillation or period. If you put a heavier kid on the same swing you would have found that the weight of the kid made no difference in the time it takes for the swing to move through one oscillation either. How can that be?

Here's the equation:

$$T = 2\pi\sqrt{\frac{L}{g}}$$

T is time, L is length of the pendulum, and g is gravity. You'll recall from above that gravity equals 9.8 m/sec/sec on earth.

Test it out. Make a pendulum. You can use a swing outside or you can use a string and a washer.

1. Tie the string to the washer and then the other end of the string to a pencil or a craft stick. Secure the stick to the backs of two chairs and suspend the washer between them.
2. Start the pendulum swinging. Time how long it takes the pendulum to swing from the upper end of one oscillation and back. It is easiest and most accurate to time ten swings and then divide the result by ten (just move the decimal one place to the left).
3. Mathematically find the length of your string using the pendulum equation from above.
4. Now measure the length of your string in meters. Give yourself a few decimals of leeway plus or minus, because your measuring of the string won't be perfect and your timing won't be perfect either.

How did it turn out? At what point in the swing does the pendulum have the maximum potential energy? At what point does it have the maximum kinetic energy? How does the swinging of a pendulum show that kinetic energy equals potential energy?

Additional Layer

These experiments all focus on movement energy, but potential energy can be chemical too. Think about a car sitting still. It has no kinetic energy, but lots of potential energy or it would never move. Where is the potential energy stored?

Famous Folks

Galileo Galilei was the first to examine the properties of pendulums. Galileo discovered that the length of the pendulum is the only factor that affects the time it takes for the pendulum to swing.

Though Galileo realized this would make pendulums useful as timekeepers, it was Christiaan Huygens of the Dutch Republic who invented the first pendulum clock, replacing sundials and hourglasses.

THE ARTS: ROMANTIC ART I

Explanation

The Romantic Art Movement was the first one to spread across continents and across genres: poetry, fiction, music, philosophy, and painting.

It was a movement of revolutionaries, people who were staunch individualists. They believed in rights, freedom of expression, the force of nature, and deep emotions. These were the ideas they tried to convey. Because it was about individualism and emotion, there was no unifying style. This period was also the first time that art was used to teach people to care about and be cognizant of each other. Artists highlighted individuals and promoted their freedom and worth.

Additional Layer

The word "Romantic" as used here actually stems from the popularity of medieval adventure tales like the Holy Grail and the legends of King Arthur. They were called romances because they were written in Romance languages.

The Romantic Period (1800-1880) is one of the most difficult art movements to precisely describe. Romantic artists didn't just paint one type of subject or in one type of style. They were trying to capture certain emotions, and they did this in all sorts of ways. The poet Charles Beudelaire said, "Romanticism is precisely situated neither in choice of subject nor in exact truth, but in a way of feeling." That feeling is what the artists were trying to capture.

This is "The Fighting Temeraire" by J.M.W. Turner. It symbolizes the end of the era of tall sailing ships and the rule of the British on the seas and the beginning of the Industrial Revolution. It is both nostalgic and proud.

Something important to note is that the word "romantic" isn't based on the word "romance" when we're talking about the Romantic Period. This art isn't about the kind of emotion that comes with hearts, flowers, or Valentine's Day. Romance in this case means glorification. Romantic artists glorified huge themes like these:

- heroism
- hope
- liberty
- spirituality
- democracy
- instinct
- nature
- survival
- despair

Notice that these words come attached to emotions. We all feel something different and very individual because we've all had different experiences. Romantic artists hoped to capture some of those emotions with their paintings.

Nature was an especially important aspect of painting during the Romantic Movement. Artists focused on how powerful nature is, and how puny people are in contrast. Romanticism is filled with paintings of storms, shipwrecks, animals, volcanoes, fires, blizzards, and other natural disasters.

Current events of the day played a large role. This was a time in history when revolutions were happening all over. The common man was rising up against their oppressors and claiming their rights and freedoms. They celebrated independence, democracy, and liberty.

😊 😊 😊 EXPLORATION: William Blake

Meet William Blake. He was an English artist. He didn't just paint though. He also wrote poetry. He wasn't very well known during his lifetime, but he is now considered to be one of the greatest men in Britain. Not everything he wrote about and painted is celebrated though. Much of what he wrote contradicted basic morals, especially in the traditional time he lived in. He saw marriage as unnecessary (though he did marry), and argued with many scientists and philosophers of his day. He supported the revolutions being fought, but in the same breath, disagreed with the men leading them.

This portrait of Blake is by Thomas Phillips and was done in 1807.

William Blake was not always understood, but he was a very deep thinker nonetheless. He never took things at face value. He changed his mind often, but never because someone told him to. He saw things from many sides and constantly wondered.

As far as his work, he painted many things based on literary works – Greek myths, Bible stories, Dante's Divine Comedy, and Mary Wollstonecraft's writings (among others). Here is a painting called *The Great Red Dragon and the Woman Clothed with Sun.* It's his interpretation Revelation 12:3-4 from the New Testament.

Explanation

The Romantic Movement was much more than just painting. It infiltrated many aspects of thought, society, and culture.

In this unit we'll examine Romantic painters and styles of painting during this period. In Unit 4-4 we'll look at other kinds of Romantic art, including music, poetry, and literature.

Fabulous Fact

The Romantic Movement lacked a unifying style, technique, or subject matter, but it can be summed up in 3 points:

Emotion

Nature

Current events

Teaching Tip

As you're introducing a new art movement, go search in art books or online for examples of paintings from the movement. Discuss them one by one and find similarities. Notice art principles and themes. Point them out to your kids. The more you practice, the better you'll get at it.

Revelation 12:3-4

3. And there appeared another wonder in heaven; and behold a great red dragon, having seven heads and ten horns, and seven crowns upon his heads.

4. And his tail drew the third part of the stars of heaven, and did cast them to the earth: and the dragon stood before the woman which was ready to be delivered, for to devour her child as soon as it was born.

Writer's Workshop

Blake considered himself a spiritual man, but not necessarily a religious one, and he certainly did not agree with the king forcing people to join the Church of England. He had his own ideas and was not easily swayed by popular opinions of his day.

What is the difference between spirituality and religion? Do you need one to have the other? Have you ever met anyone who is religious, but not spiritual (or vice versa). Do the two ever co-exist? Can you be spiritual, but lack morals?

Write about your ideas in your writer's notebook.

He is known for painting scenes from many literary works, so to remember him, choose a favorite book of your own and make a work of art featuring one of its scenes. It could be from scripture, from a poem you like, or from a contemporary story you enjoy. Choose a scene from the story that is filled with emotion - fear, anger, hurt, joy, surprise, or loneliness. Paint that scene to show an emotion as the Romantics would have. For example, if I were to paint a scene from *Charlotte's Web* I may choose to show the elation Wilbur felt when he won the ribbon at the fair. If I were to paint a scene from the *Harry Potter* series, I might choose the one when Harry realizes he must die as he's walking into the Forbidden Forest to face Voldemort, with fear, but also determination in his steps. If I chose a scripture story, it may be the relief and power of Moses as he has just parted the Red Sea to help the people escape slavery in Egypt. Choose a scene that makes you feel something, and it will be easier for you to paint the emotion.

☺ ☺ ☺ EXPLORATION: Constable's Cloudscape

John Constable started painting when he was a youngster in school. He spent his childhood in the English countryside, the son of a wealthy businessman. He loved to go hiking and almost always brought his sketchbook and watercolors along. Several members of his family and also several friendly neighbors of his were painters, and they encouraged him in his arts. He became one of the greatest landscape painters of all time, perhaps partly because he always painted what he loved best – the fields, farms, hills, and sea near his home. He also painted beautiful skies and breathtaking, realistic clouds.

This painting by Constable is called "Extensive Landscape With Grey Clouds" and was painted in 1821.

When the focus of a painting is the sky, we call it a cloudscape. You can make your own cloudscape.

1. Go outside with a pencil and thick watercolor paper and sketch the clouds lightly with pencil. Tape the paper on to a table or board using long strips of masking tape so the paper is completely attached down on all four sides. Once the border is marked out, continue your sketch around the bottom edge. Add some simple trees, bushes, and hills.
2. To make a light sky blue color with watercolors, mix dark blue paint with quite a bit of water in a dish or in the cover of the paint tray. Mix up lots of blue paint so you are certain not to run out of the shade.
3. Quickly wash over all the sky areas of your painting with the blue paint. Use a large brush on the open areas and a small-

Additional Layer

When asked what inspired him most, John Constable said, "The sound of water escaping from mill dams, willows, old rotten planks, slimy posts, and brickwork. I love such things. These scenes made me a painter."

What things inspire you?

Make a list at the front of your sketchbook of things that inspire you. What do you find beautiful? Soothing? Thought-provoking? Include all those things on your list.

Additional Layer

Constable was English, but his art inspired a group of French artists who gathered at Barbizon, a small village in France, to paint in his style. The Barbizon School painted landscapes, animals, and nature. Carot, Daubigny, Diaz, Millet, Decamps, and Rousseau were there, among others. Later more artists would come to paint in this area and make a name for themselves as they ushered in Impressionism, notably Claude Monet, Pierre-Auguste Renoir, Alfred Sisley, and Frederic Bazille.

Watercolor Tips

Use high quality watercolor paper, not just card stock and definitely not printer paper. Watercolor paper is thick and has the perfect absorbency for watercolors.

Really work your watercolor paints with a wet brush before you ever start painting. The paint should be very incorporated into the water so it is vibrant instead of just runny.

When you're dabbing the clouds, you have to absorb off the paint before it dries or else you won't be able to get the white cloud effect. Sometimes it helps if you get your dabbing napkin a tiny bit wet before dabbing if the painting has dried too much. You can also paint over it with a plain wet brush again (no extra paint, just water) before dabbing.

Fabulous Fact

Gericault visited hospitals to see sick and dying people firsthand, interviewed several survivors of the tragedy, and even made a model raft before painting the *Medusa*.

er brush around the trees and hills. Work really quickly, and before the paint has a chance to dry or soak in, use tissues to pat out several white clouds. The tissue will soak up the paint, showing the white paper underneath and leaving a blurry edge between white and blue, just like in real clouds.

4. Let the sky dry completely.
5. Once it's dry, paint the rest of your scene. Add the hills, bushes, trees, and other details you decided to add in. Let it dry again, then remove the masking tape and the paper will have a crisp, white border on it.

☺ ☺ ☺ EXPLORATION: The Raft of the Medusa

The oil painting on the next page is by Theodore Gericault. It is huge (over 16 feet by 23 feet) and depicts a terrible scene.

Anyone in the day already knew the story of the French naval frigate, the *Medusa*. Poor navigation had brought it over a hundred miles off course when it ran aground. A hastily built raft was constructed because there weren't enough lifeboats. At least 147 people had boarded the slipshod craft; all but 15 died before they were finally rescued thirteen days later. The survivors endured starvation, dehydration, and cannibalism before the rescue. It was quite a scandal. And even though King Louis XVII had no say in the incompetent naval captain's appointment, he got the rap for it. Having just been restored to the throne, the people were watching for him to make mistakes.

How is size important in art? Would Gericault's painting have the same effect on a small scale? What do you think he wanted people to feel when they saw his painting of this terrible scene?

Teaching Tip

Point out that *The Raft of the Medusa* is an example of the Romantic idea that nature is more powerful than man. It is also a clear example of protest art, as Gericault was making a social statement. Only the wealthiest were given space on the lifeboats, while the lower class people became the victims of this horrible tragedy.

Read today's newspaper or look up a news story from the Internet. Find a current tragedy happening in the world today. Make it the subject matter of an oversized painting. Use a roll of butcher paper cut to at least 6 feet. Begin by sketching the scene of the tragedy, then fill it in with paints. Fill the whole paper.

How does size impact your painting? Were you able to make a statement along with just portraying an event? Is there emotion within your scene?

☺ ☺ ☺ EXPLORATION: Lion Attacking A Horse

George Stubbs was an English painter who was fascinated with painting animals. He had a profound respect for nature, regarding it as the most superior art. No one ever found his journals, sketchbooks, or letters, so we don't know much at all about his life, but a few years after he died an article was published about him that told the story that supposedly inspired Stubbs to paint many versions of lions and horses. No one is really sure if the story is true or not, but the article told of Stubbs' fascination with seeing wild animals in menageries around Europe, and in particular, of one excursion to Morocco during a vacation to Italy in which Stubbs was given a chance to fulfill his dream of seeing a lion. Stubbs, atop a balcony, reportedly saw this dramatic event: "One evening, while Stubbs and his friend were viewing the delightful scenery, and a thousand beautiful objects, from this elevation, which the brilliancy of the moon rendered more interesting, a lion was observed at some distance, directing his way, with a slow pace, towards a white Barbary horse, which appeared grazing not more than two hundred yards distant from the moat [of

Writer's Workshop

Write up your own newspaper article to describe the event you read about and then painted. Remember that a newspaper article doesn't typically start at the beginning. Rather, it tells the most exciting part in the very first line, then goes back and fills in the details. Try to make your article unbiased and factual. See if you can spot any opinions or biases in the article you read in the newspaper or on the Internet.

On The Web

There are many excellent how to draw tutorials for animals on-line. Choose an animal you've always wanted to see in real life, then use a tutorial to draw one.

Additional Layer

One of the reasons critics don't believe George Stubbs really witnessed a lion attacking a horse in Morocco is because his paintings are strikingly similar to a Greek statue that was in Rome during his visit there. Chances are he was inspired by the statue, and his imagination filled in the blanks as he created his series of paintings of the horse and lion.

Go visit https://youtu.be/Qn6tsoooRM to see the amazing statue's installation in the Getty Museum.

Writer's Workshop

Would you rather paint real things you've seen, or things from your imagination? Write about it and tell why you feel the way you do.

the private zoo]. Mr. Stubbs was reminded of the gratification he had so often wished for. The orb of night was perfectly clear, and the horizon serene. The lion did not make towards the horse by a regular approach, but performed many curvatures, still drawing nearer towards the devoted animal, till the lion, by the shelter of a rocky situation, came suddenly upon his prey. The affrighted barb beheld his enemy, and, as if conscious of his fate, threw himself into an attitude highly interesting to the painter. The noble creature then appeared fascinated, and the lion, finding him within his power, sprang in a moment, like a cat, on the back of the defenseless horse, threw him down, and instantly tore out his bowels" (The Sporting Magazine, May 1808).

Many say he was never in Morocco at all, but whether or not he saw a lion attacking a horse in real life, the image was somehow important and lingered in his mind. He painted it over and over again, making many versions of the lion and the horse. He identified with the horse's innocence and purity, as shown by its light color. The painting definitely shows off the Romantic idea of the power and destructive ability of nature.

Stubbs visited menageries and watched live animals. He even dissected horses so he could better understand their anatomy as he painted. With your sketchbook, observe a live animal. Sketch the animal as you watch it. As you do so, also take notes about its behavior, characteristics, and your overall impression of the animal. Try to incorporate some emotion into your picture. Color is an important tool in communicating emotion. For example, the horse in the painting is white, seeming pure and innocent. The lion's dark shading gives it a sneaky, strong, and malicious feel. The dark, muted scenery casts a feeling of gloom and fear. What colors can help you communicate the emotion of the animal you drew?

☺ ☺ ☺ **EXPLORATION: Liberty Leading the People**
Eugene Delacroix painted the scene below in honor of the French Revolution. At the time, every person who saw this painting knew about this pivotal historical event.

It showed the people rising up against oppression, led by the idea of liberty. It was an ideal worth dying for and worth killing for.

The painting shows sacrifice and a healthy amount of hope. Notice where the light and dark are portrayed in the painting. What ideas are represented by darkness? Which are represented by light?

When we see the Statue of Liberty, we can feel some of these same emotions the author wanted Frenchmen to feel when he painted this. The Statue of Liberty represents the hope that comes with liberty and our ability to rise up and make our own way in the world. Draw and paint your own lady liberty.

Famous Folks

Eugene Delacroix was the leader of the French Romantic School. He was inspired by great writers like William Shakespeare, Lord Byron, and Walter Scott. He was also a talented lithographer and illustrated some of Shakespeare's works. This is his self portrait.

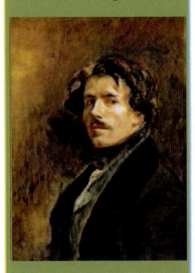

Explanation

The Romantic Period was, no doubt, a time of revolutions and changes in the politics of the world. Artists used their art to stand up for what they believed in. They protested current events, wars, and overstepping governments The difficulty was finding an audience to buy their political statements. Their positions were often appreciated, but not necessarily marketable.

1. Look at pictures of the Statue of Liberty to use as a reference. Don't use pencil for this (when drawing realistic things kids can sometimes get caught up in perfection and it will take forever). Instead, use a sharpie marker and outline Lady Liberty. Mistakes are okay. Just do your best. Make sure she mostly fills the page to make her look grand and be the focal point of your picture.

2. Add her stand and island in the foreground. Draw the waterline from the harbor about halfway up the page, creating a foreground and a background.

3. Fill in the background with a cityscape. From the left to right, completely fill in the background with buildings. You can have sky peeking out behind the buildings.

4. Once your sharpie sketch is done, fill in the painting with watercolor paints. The statue itself will be the right color if you combine green watercolors with a tiny bit of black watercolors.

☻ ☺ EXPLORATION: Francisco Goya

Francisco Goya lived and painted in Madrid, Spain. He was the king's painter there, and enjoyed being a part of the royal court and its luxury. When he was about 46 years old he suddenly became deaf following a serious illness. This changed his outlook on life, and his bitterness showed through his paintings, which became darker and darker as time went on. Right about the same time he went deaf France invaded Spain, and Goya painted his most famous painting about that invasion and the war that ensued. It is called *The Third of May 1808*, a painting that shows a French firing squad killing a group of Spaniards.

Watch this video analysis of this painting by Khan Academy, and then point out and discuss the things the art critics have described.

https://www.khanacademy.org/humanities/becoming-modern/romanticism/romanticism-in-spain/v/goya-third-may

☺ ☺ ☺ EXPLORATION: Thomas Lawrence

Thomas Lawrence was unlike most of the trained painters of his day. First, he was self-taught. Second, he was a child prodigy, supporting his family with his painting by the time he was ten years old. Third, he was primarily a portrait painter, the most famous one of his day. Even when others encouraged him to paint nature and other fashionable subjects of the Romantic era, he stuck mostly with portraits, and had a knack for painting exact likenesses. This is quite a bit trickier than you might think. Today we use cameras to capture likenesses, and even then, many of the portraits don't turn out the way we'd like them to. Imagine having to quickly paint an accurate portrait of someone, especially if that someone is a queen. Lawrence's very first royally com-

Imagination was a key component of the Romantic era. The Age of Reason valued only observable facts, but the Romantics felt that definition limited the mind. Imagination was creativity; it was the potential for understanding great truths through thought and epiphany, not just observations. Romantics believed that people could use their minds, intuition, and imagination to understand truth. This was one of the first times in history when imaginary art was valued.

Sometimes the imaginary scenes were hopeful and beautiful, as in Cole's *The Voyage of Life*.

But others were dark and scary, like Henry Fuseli's *The Nightmare*.

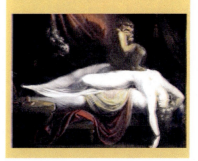

Famous Folks

J.M.W. Turner was a master of watercolor landscapes. He is called the painter of light because of his amazing ability to capture the brilliance of light in his paintings. He traveled all over Europe painting.

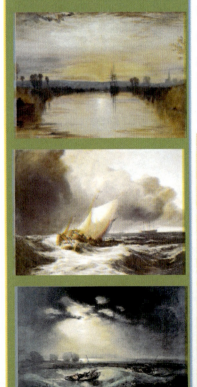

missioned portrait was of Queen Charlotte, the queen of England. He went to Windsor palace to paint the queen and Princess Amelia. Though everyone else raved over the beauty and accuracy of the queen's portrait when it was displayed, Charlotte herself never liked it. Perhaps it was just one of those cases where we tend never to be satisfied enough with our own looks.

Have someone sit for you for 30 minutes. Set up your portrait spot and get your oil paints, brushes, and canvas ready. See how well you can paint your subject while they wait, holding very still. Is it a good likeness? Is your subject happy with it? The job of a portrait artist is not an easy one.

EXPLORATION: Hudson River School

The Hudson River School was an art movement in America in the mid-1800's. It was a group of painters who painted American landscape paintings. They separated themselves from the European artists of the day and created the first school of painting in the United States. Similar to the emotional themes of Romanticism, the Hudson River School focused on themes of exploration, discovery, settlement of new areas – all things that were important in America at the time.

The paintings are realistic and serene. The painters usually went to the spot to do sketches before painting back in the studio.

The painting in this exploration is called *The Domes of the Yosemite* and is by Albert Bierstadt. Look at lots of paintings from the Hudson River School on the internet and notice not only the beauty of the paintings, but also some of the techniques. In particular, look at landscape lines that separate the foreground from

the background. Also notice how often the things in the foreground are more colorful, bright, and bold, while the things in the background look more pastel and faded to show the distance.

Make a paper collage of mountains using this idea. You'll need a variety of papers of the same hue, but different values. For example, gather papers that are all blue or all green or all purple - some light, some dark, and some in between. Once they are gathered, arrange them from dark at the front to light at the back. Beginning with the darkest color, cut a mountain-scape shape. Glue it down to the next sheet, and then cut a different mountain-scape shape from that one. Glue it down to the next in the stack, and continue until you have glued them all down to the very back sheet. You can choose a different color for your back sheet; this one is backed with gray. If you choose to do green mountains you may want to back it with a blue skyline.

Now look at the paintings from the Hudson River School again. Can you find this pattern of dark to light in any of them? Can you see how things appear to be further away as they fade? What else do you notice that the Hudson River artists do to make their landscapes seem to have depth and look realistic? How are these American landscape paintings different than the European landscapes that we've seen during the Romantic Period?

😊 😊 😊 EXPLORATION: Caspar David Friedrich
Caspar David Friedrich was a German painter. He was a bit of a loner. He was confident though, and definitely talented. Unlike other European artists at the time, he did not join in a school or

On The Web

Watch this video about the Hudson River School by art historian, Linda S. Ferber.

https://youtu.be/MWEoNSpcttk

On the Web

Get a set of free printable Hudson River School art cards from Layers of Learning here:

http://www.layers-of-learning.com/hudson-river-school-art-cards/

Fabulous Fact

The Hudson River School got its name because some of the first members drew their inspiration from the Catskill region of New York where the Hudson River flows.

Explanation

The works from the Hudson River School helped to settle more of America. Because the painters made it look so beautiful, people weren't as afraid of the wilderness land anymore. After World War I Hudson River School paintings surged in popularity again because they represented the beauty of America and were a symbol of strength and patriotism.

Additional Layer

This painting of Tintern Abbey perfectly showcases the Romantic idea that nature is an unstoppable power. J.M.W. Turner painted this monastery. It was founded in 1131, but left to decay for several centuries. The man-made building was retaken by nature, as you can see by the vines growing all over its walls. The idea is that eventually anything we create can be taken back by the natural world.

Many Romantic artists and poets were inspired by this beautiful, but haunting abbey. Turner visited it twice before painting it. William Wordsworth also visited the spot and then wrote a famous poem about it called *Lines Composed a Few Miles above Tintern Abbey*.

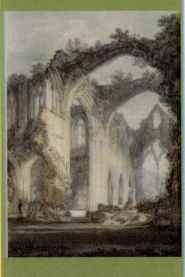

get together with other artists to paint and collaborate. He just painted, not feeling the need to be inspired by other painters or learn from like-minded artists. He saw painting as a peaceful way to worship God rather than as a social engagement. This is Friedrich in his studio, painted by another artist friend named Georg Friedrich Kersting.

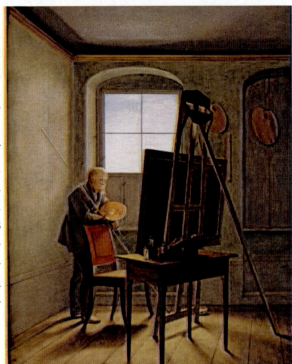

Though he was not the most famous of the Romantic painters, many say that Caspar David Friedrich painted the quintessential Romantic painting, *Wanderer Above the Sea of Fog*.

As you look at this painting, discuss these things:

1. The power of nature versus the insignificance of man. This rocky precipice would make the man seem like he's almost on top of the world, but no matter where man is, nature is bigger. Man's glory, no matter how wealthy or full of status or position, will always bow to nature's.
2. Our inability to see the man's face makes us wonder - is he sad? Afraid? Excited? Awestruck? Joyful? How would you feel atop that overlook by yourself? Can you picture yourself in the place of the man? Would you be able to as easily if you could see the man's face?
3. The use of line in this painting. Notice how our eyes are drawn to the solitary man by the diagonal horizon lines pointing toward him.
4. This painting was done vertically rather than horizontally, which was unusual for the time. This makes the man seem even more upright and tall.

In your sketchbook, lightly draw a triangle towards the bottom mimicking the triangular rock precipice. Add diagonal lines heading toward a central vanishing point. Now sketch a picture of a person standing from the back directly in the center. Fill in the details of the sketch any way you wish. You could be looking over farmland, a sea, a desert, or a garden.

Additional Layer

Friedrich felt that solitude combined with nature would lead to spirituality. His favorite things to paint were scenes at dawn and at sunset. He loved to play with the look of the sun's rays.

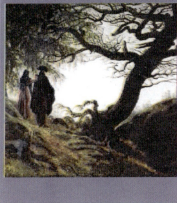

Coming up next . . .

Unit 4-4

Revolutions
Mountain West States
Energy Sources
Romantic Art II

Spinning Jenny

The woman in this picture is using a yarn producing machine called a spinning jenny. This was one of the most important machines of the early Industrial Revolution. It was invented in 1764 by Englishman James Hargreaves because a man called John Kay had invented a faster way to weave cloth, but the people who prepared the yarn by hand couldn't keep up with the new weaving machines. The two machines made the production of cotton yarn lucrative. They also threated the jobs of home weavers and spinners. Some of the people became frightened enough to smash up some of the cotton mills and Hargreaves' home.

Industrial Revolution: Unit 4-3

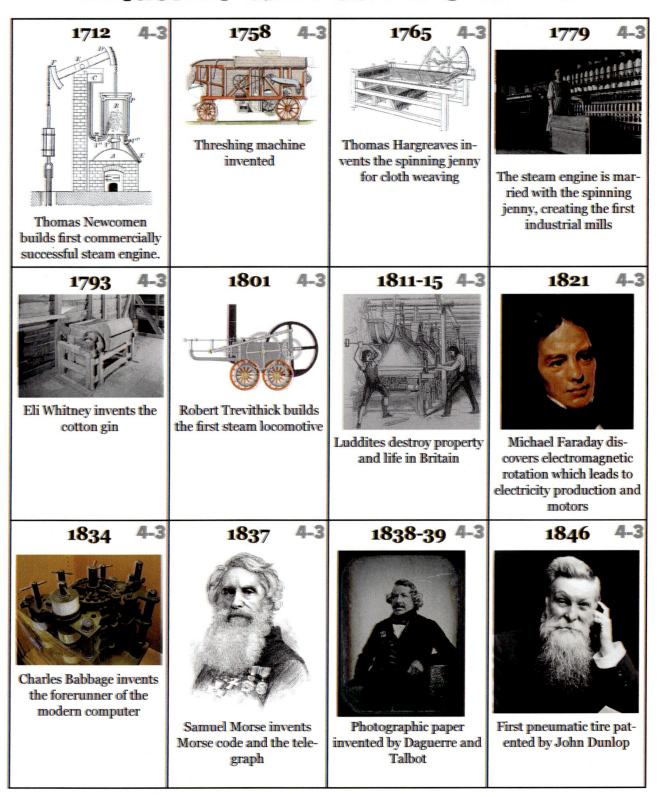

1712 4-3

Thomas Newcomen builds first commercially successful steam engine.

1758 4-3

Threshing machine invented

1765 4-3

Thomas Hargreaves invents the spinning jenny for cloth weaving

1779 4-3

The steam engine is married with the spinning jenny, creating the first industrial mills

1793 4-3

Eli Whitney invents the cotton gin

1801 4-3

Robert Trevithick builds the first steam locomotive

1811-15 4-3

Luddites destroy property and life in Britain

1821 4-3

Michael Faraday discovers electromagnetic rotation which leads to electricity production and motors

1834 4-3

Charles Babbage invents the forerunner of the modern computer

1837 4-3

Samuel Morse invents Morse code and the telegraph

1838-39 4-3

Photographic paper invented by Daguerre and Talbot

1846 4-3

First pneumatic tire patented by John Dunlop

1846 4-3
Transatlantic cable laid

1850 4-3
Process for refining petroleum first invented by James Young

1851 4-3
Isaac Singer invents his sewing machine

1859 4-3
Oil is first struck in Pennsylvania

1867 4-3
Alfred Nobel invents dynamite

1879 4-3
Thomas Edison invents the light bulb

1883 4-3
The first skyscraper is built in Chicago

1883 4-3
The Brooklyn Bridge is the largest suspension bridge ever built

1885 4-3
Benz invents the internal combustion engine and puts it on a carriage

1901 4-3
Marconi first transmits radio signals wirelessly

1903 4-3
Wright Brothers take first powered flight

1906 4-3
Henry Ford mass produces the automobile

Capitalism and Cronyism

An economic system where people are free to control their own property, including their labor. They are also responsible for the outcome of their choices.

People must voluntarily choose to be honest, compassionate, and careful of resources. If coercion is needed they are no longer free.

Exchanging goods freely makes everyone more wealthy and automatically becomes the most efficient use of all resources.

The government must be powerful enough to protect the rights of its citizens from abuse, but not so large that it controls their lives.

Money must be counted on to retain its value over time so that people can save and invest in the future.

People who can think creatively and critically are essential for economic growth and the maintenance of freedom.

An economic system where individuals freely own property, but government is heavily used to skew markets and control economic behavior.

In order to control people you have to have a great deal of money, military, and manpower.

When people can no longer make moral decisions for themselves they have to be controlled. Also, lack of morals leads to corrupt government.

People who do not think critically or have a correct understanding of facts cannot protect themselves from clever villains in business or government.

The word rectangles below are in random order. Cut them out and match them to the definitions on the "Capitalism and Cronyism" page. Glue each definition along the top edge of the rectangle so it creates a flap you can open to read the definition underneath. A key with answers is on page 14.

Capitalism	Cronyism	Virtue
Intrusive Government	Free Trade	Stable Currency
Small Government	Greed & Dishonesty	Educated Citizens
Ignorant Citizens		

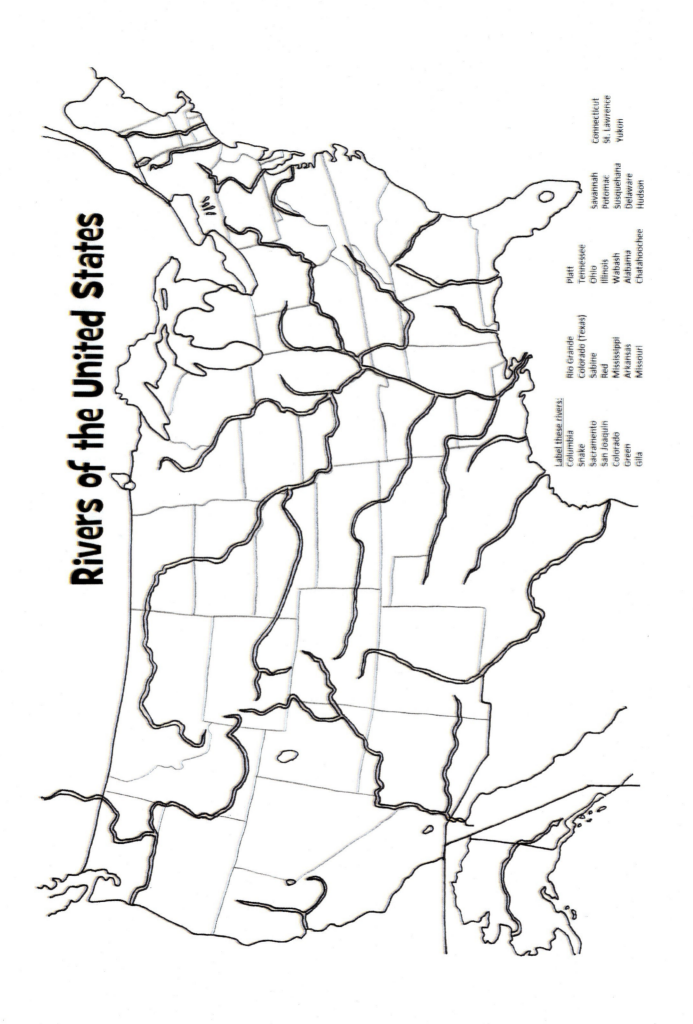

Rivers of the United States

Label these rivers:
Columbia
Snake
Sacramento
San Joaquin
Colorado
Green
Gila

Rio Grande
Colorado (Texas)
Sabine
Red
Mississippi
Arkansas
Missouri

Platt
Tennessee
Ohio
Illinois
Wabash
Alabama
Chatahoochee

Savannah
Potomac
Susquehana
Delaware
Hudson

Connecticut
St. Lawrence
Yukon

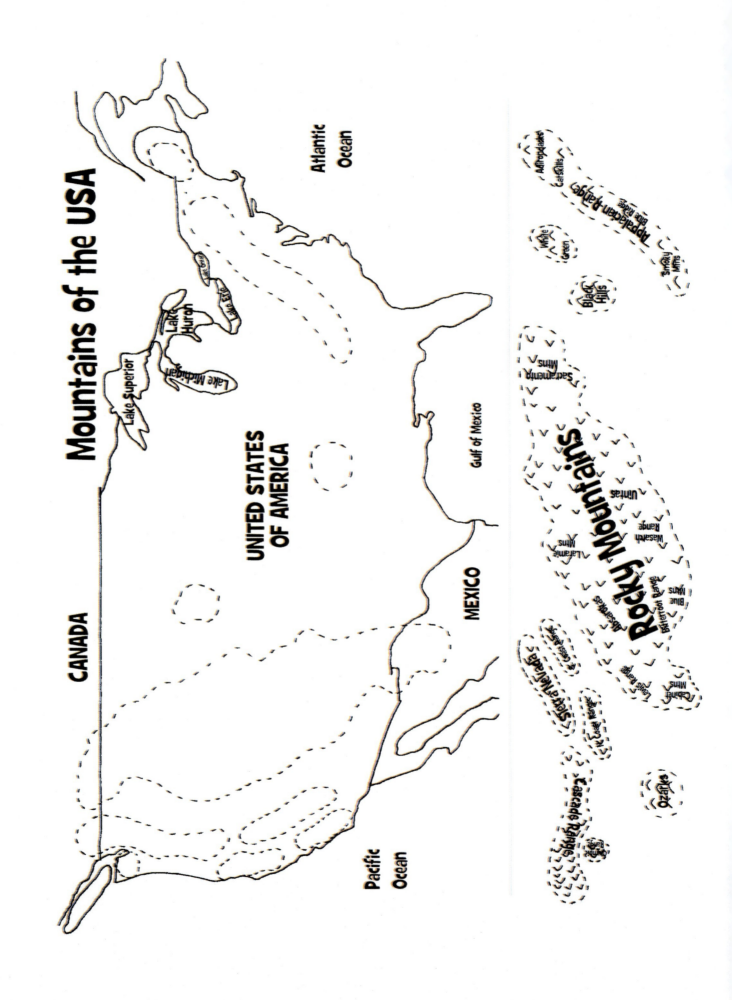

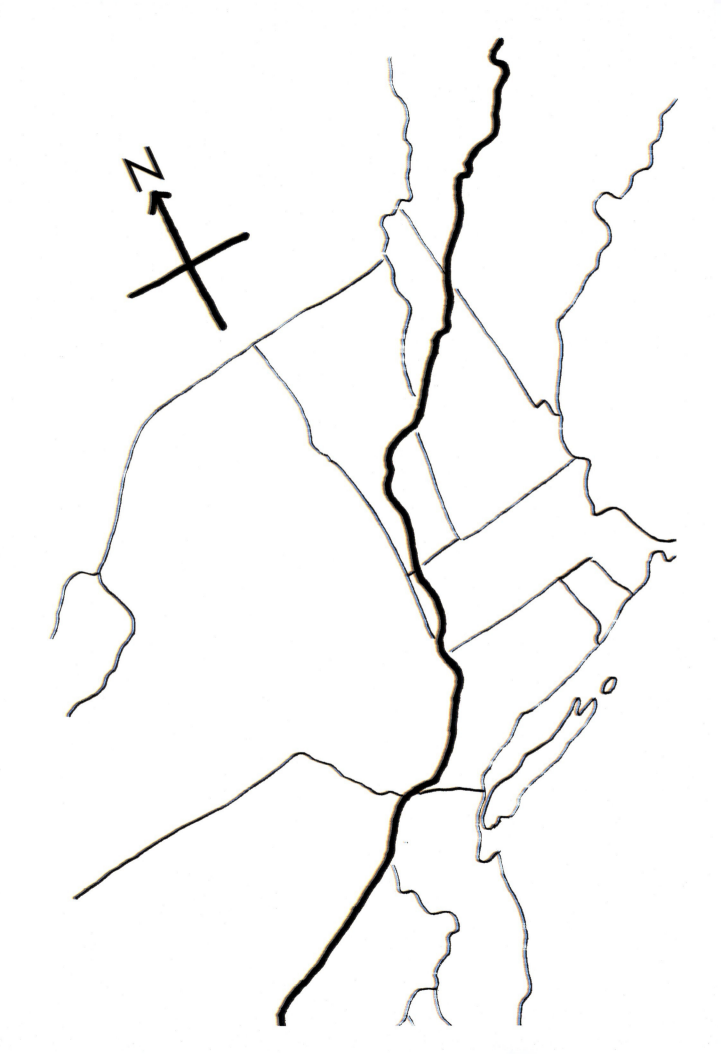

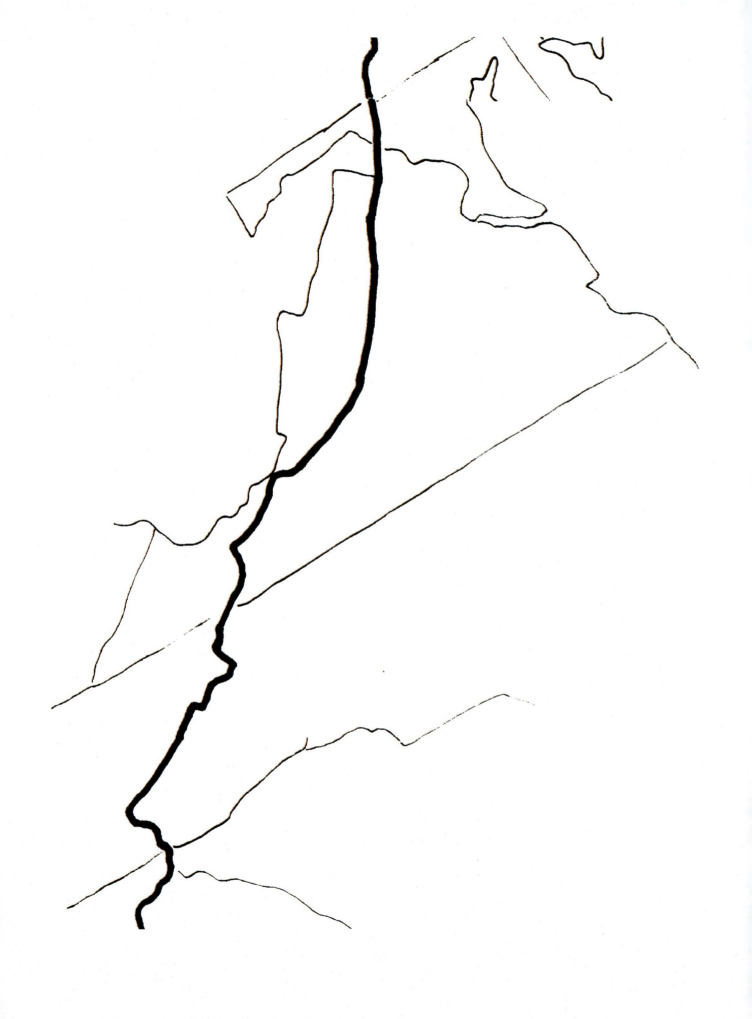

Appalachian Trail

Animal Life		
Plant Life		

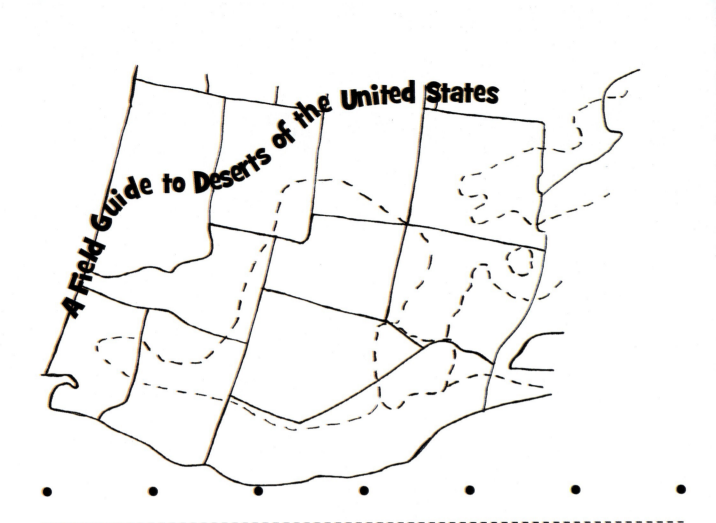

A Field Guide to Deserts of the United States

About the Authors

Karen & Michelle . . .
Mothers, sisters, teachers, women who are passionate
about educating kids.
We are dedicated to lifelong learning.

Karen, a mother of four, who has homeschooled her kids for more than eight years with her husband, Bob, has a bachelor's degree in child development with an emphasis in education. She lives in Idaho, gardens, teaches piano, and plays an excruciating number of board games with her kids. Karen is our resident arts expert and English guru {most necessary as Michelle regularly and carelessly mangles the English language and occasionally steps over the bounds of polite society}.

Michelle and her husband, Cameron, have homeschooled their six boys for more than a decade. Michelle earned a bachelors in biology, making her the resident science expert, though she is mocked by her friends for being the Botanist with the Black Thumb of Death. She also is the go-to for history and government. She believes in staying up late, hot chocolate, and a no whining policy. We both pitch in on geography, in case you were wondering, and are on a continual quest for knowledge.

Visit our constantly updated blog for tons of free ideas,
free printables, and more cool stuff for sale:
www.Layers-of-Learning.com

Made in the USA
Las Vegas, NV
28 July 2023